Nelson's Electronic Bible Reference Library USER'S GUIDE

D1010395

NelsonElectronic PUBLISHING

P.O. Box 141000, Nashville, TN 37214

Nelson's Electronic Bible Reference Library, Running Logos Library System Version 2.1

SOFTWARE LICENSE AGREEMENT

CAREFULLY READ THE FOLLOWING TERMS AND CONDITIONS BEFORE USING THIS SOFTWARE. USING THIS SOFTWARE INDICATES YOUR ACCEPTANCE OF THESE TERMS AND CONDITIONS. IF YOU ARE NOT IN AGREEMENT, PROMPTLY RETURN THE SOFTWARE PACKAGE UNUSED WITH YOUR RECEIPT AND YOUR MONEY WILL BE REFUNDED.

LICENSE

The SOFTWARE may be used only on a single machine at a time. This is a copyrighted software program and may not be copied, duplicated, or distributed except for the purpose of backup by the licensed owner.

The SOFTWARE may be copied into any machine-readable or printed form for backup, modification, or normal usage in support of the SOFTWARE on the single machine.

You may transfer the SOFTWARE and license to another party if the other party agrees to accept the terms and conditions of this Agreement. If you transfer the SOFTWARE, you must either transfer all copies, whether in printed or machine-readable form, to the same party or destroy any copies not transferred; this includes all modifications and portions of the SOFTWARE contained or merged into other software and/or software programs.

YOU MAY NOT USE, COPY, ALTER OR OTHERWISE MODIFY, OR TRANSFER THE SOFTWARE OR DATABASE(S) OR ANY ADD-ON PRODUCT'S TEXT EXCEPT AS EXPRESSLY PROVIDED FOR IN THIS LICENSE.

IF YOU TRANSFER POSSESSION OF ANY COPY OR MODIFICATIONS OF THE SOFTWARE TO ANOTHER PARTY, EXCEPT AS EXPRESSLY PROVIDED FOR IN THIS LICENSE, YOUR LICENSE THEREUPON IS AUTOMATICALLY TERMINATED.

LIMITED SOFTWARE WARRANTY

LIMITED WARRANTY. *Nelson Electronic Publishing* warrants that, for ninety (90) days from the date of receipt, the computer programs contained in the SOFTWARE will perform substantially in accordance with the accompanying *User's Guide.* Any implied warranties on the SOFTWARE are limited to ninety (90) days. Some jurisdictions do not allow limitations on the duration of an implied warranty, so the above limitation may not apply to you.

CUSTOMER REMEDIES. *Nelson Electronic Publishing's* entire liability and your exclusive remedy shall be, at our option, either (a) return of the price paid or (b) repair or replacement of SOFTWARE that does not meet *Nelson Electronic Publishing's* Limited Warranty and that is returned to us with a copy of your receipt. This Limited Warranty is void if failure of the SOFTWARE has resulted from accident, abuse, or misapplication. Any replacement SOFTWARE will be warranted for the remainder of the original warranty period or thirty (30) days, whichever is longer. Outside the United States, neither these remedies nor any product support services are available without proof of purchase from an authorized non-U.S. source.

NO OTHER WARRANTIES. To the maximum extent permitted by applicable law, *Nelson Electronic Publishing* and its suppliers disclaim all other warranties, either expressed or implied, including, but not limited to, implied warranties of merchantability and fitness for a particular purpose, with regard to the SOFTWARE and the accompanying written materials. This Limited Warranty gives you specific legal rights. You may have others, which vary from state to state.

NO LIABILITY FOR CONSEQUENTIAL DAMAGES. TO THE MAXIMUM EXTENT PERMITTED BY APPLICABLE LAW, IN NO EVENT SHALL *NELSON ELECTRONIC PUBLISHING* OR ITS SUPPLIERS BE LIABLE FOR ANY DAMAGES WHATSOEVER (INCLUDING WITHOUT LIMITATION, DAMAGES FOR LOSS OF BUSINESS PROFITS, BUSINESS INTERRUPTION, LOSS OF BUSINESS INFORMATION, OR ANY OTHER PECUNIARY LOSS) ARISING OUT OF THE USE OF OR INABILITY TO USE THIS PRODUCT, EVEN IF *NELSON ELECTRONIC PUBLISHING* HAS BEEN ADVISED OF THE POSSIBILITY OF SUCH DAMAGES. BECAUSE SOME STATES DO NOT ALLOW THE EXCLUSION OF LIABILITY FOR CONSEQUENTIAL OR ACCIDENTAL DAMAGES, THE ABOVE LIMITATION MAY NOT APPLY TO YOU.

Should you have any questions concerning this Agreement, please contact:

Nelson Electronic Publishing
Thomas Nelson, Inc.
501 Nelson Place
Nashville, TN 37214-1000
615/889-9000

User's Guide
Nelson's Electronic Bible Reference Library
(Running the Logos Library System Version 2.1)

Nelson Electronic Publishing Headquarters and Distributors

USA: **THOMAS NELSON, INC.**
Address: 501 Nelson Place, Nashville, TN 37214-1000; Unlock & Sales: (800) 933-9673 x2830; Unlock & Sales Fax: (800) 308-6793; Sales Internet: http://www.NelsonWordDirect.com; Sales Email: NelsonWordDirect@ThomasNelson.com; Tech Support Phone: (615) 902-2440; Tech Support Fax: (615) 902-2450; Technical Email: NelsonCDTech@ThomasNelson.com

Hours:	Mon	8:00 a.m.–8:00 p.m.
	Tue	8:00 a.m.–8:00 p.m.
	Wed	8:00 a.m.–5:00 p.m.
	Thu	8:00 a.m.–8:00 p.m.
	Fri	8:00 a.m.–5:00 p.m.
	Sat	9:00 a.m.–1:00 p.m.

Canada: **WORD ENTERTAINMENT**, 7720 Alderbridge Way, Richmond, BC V6X-2A2, CANADA; Phone: (800) 663-3133

England: **WORD ENTERTAINMENT**, 9 Holdom Avenue, Bletchley, Milton Keynes, MK1 QR, ENGLAND; Phone: 011-44-1908-648-440

Australia: **KOORONG BOOKS**, 28 West Parade, West Ryde, NSW 2114 AUSTRALIA; Phone: 612-9857-4477

WORD AUSTRALIA, 142 Canterbury, Kilsyth, VIC 3137 AUSTRALIA; Phone: 613-9729-3777

BIBLE SOCIETY IN AUSTRALIA, 30 York Road, Ingleburn, NSW 2565 AUSTRALIA; Phone: 612-9605-7822

New Zealand: **BIBLE SOCIETY OF NEW ZEALAND**, Marion Square, Wellington, NEW ZEALAND; Phone: 644-384-4119

South Africa: **LOGOS INFORMATION SYSTEMS**, P.O. Box 48993, Roosevelt Park, Johannesburg, 2129 SOUTH AFRICA; Phone: 11-782-4488

Publisher's Preface

Welcome to *Nelson's Electronic Bible Reference Library*! You have purchased the most powerful and expandable library system on the market and stocked it with books from the world's leading publisher of Bibles and biblical reference material. We hope that it brings you many fruitful and fulfilling hours of study and enjoyment, and equips you to understand and share the Word of God like never before!

Read through the rest of this guide for a quick overview of the most useful and powerful features of *Nelson's Electronic Bible Reference Library* (NEBRL). The software engine behind this remarkable collection is the latest version (2.1) of the Logos Bible Software and the Logos Library System™ (LLS), the leading standard for electronic publishing. It provides powerful, yet easy to use software, and allows you to quickly, easily, and economically add additional books to your library as your needs change.

Nelson's Electronic Bible Reference Library (NEBRL) contains the complete LLS technology. Nothing is missing. The LLS opens this unmatched collection from Nelson along with any other books sharing the LLS standard, regardless of the publisher. Now you can stock your electronic library with the best books from Thomas Nelson, and identify others that are guaranteed to work seamlessly with NEBRL by looking for the LLS logo where you buy electronic books.

Philip P. Stoner
Vice President & Publisher, Nelson Reference & Electronic Publishing

Developer's Preface

This new version of The Logos Library System (Version 2.1) has been designed and written to enhance personal Bible study. At Logos Research Systems we believe that quality software tools, Bible texts, and reference works make the Bible more accessible as well as facilitate its study. We thank all of our loyal users who have been gracious with their time and suggestions to assist us in making this new generation of The Logos Library System the unparalleled biblical library tool that it has become. We are committed to a vigorous ongoing program of research and development which will ensure the continuing technical superiority of these tools, and toward this end we welcome your comments and suggestions.

Dale Pritchett
Vice President, Sales and Marketing

Contents

1
What's New?

Introduction

Welcome to the *Nelson's Electronic Bible Reference Library!*

Nelson's Electronic Bible Reference Library (NEBRL), which uses Logos Research Systems' Logos Library System (LLS) brings together books of all kinds into an integrated library system, with hyperlink cross-references, topical browsing, note-taking, and above all, powerful, multi-book searching. The integration of many reference works in the Library enables users to search for combinations of information that were never before possible apart from weeks or months of laborious effort. Added electronic enhancements make even the most complex material accessible, easier and more efficient to use than printed editions.

Designed to display any and all written languages, modern and ancient, The Logos Library System is one of the world's first multilingual, multimedia, hypertext engines. Moreover, all LLS books are language-aware, enabling true multilingual searching.

Our goal is to create a library system that is easy for the novice to use profitably and yet powerful enough to meet the needs of the most advanced professional.

NEBRL Key Features

Nelson's Electronic Bible Reference Library (NEBRL) is designed to bring the library to the student instead of the student to the library. Unlike traditional Bible software, NEBRL is designed from the ground up to be a universal search, retrieval, and note-taking system for all kinds of books and data, including Bibles, commentaries, dictionaries, encyclopedias, atlases, videos, recordings, charts, and diagrams.

- **Microsoft Windows 3.1 and Windows 95 compatible:** All Nelson and Logos software products are fully state-of-the-art with the latest advances in Windows technology.

- **Virtually unlimited capacity:** Economically build a library of hundreds of volumes, limited only by hardware capacity. With a notebook computer and a CD-ROM drive you can truly hold an entire library in your hand.

■ **Automated Library Management:** NEBRL offers a large set of categories and subcategories to accommodate a library. Categories and individual books are accessed through a unique "Library Browser" giving you instant access across categories, books, and multilayered tables of content. Individual books contain full text, graphics, photos, publisher's typographic style, as well as full motion video and stereo sound. Full Library of Congress "MARC" records are maintained internally for future linkage to other services.

■ **Seamless Integration:** Add and delete books according to individual taste. This is your library. Choose the books according to your own taste. Books may be purchased as collections or individual volumes.

■ **Search and Link Across Multiple Books:** When you perform a search or even read a book, you have interactivity between all books in the library.

■ **Transparent Support for Multiple Drives:** NEBRL provides support for multiple hard drives and multiple CD-ROMS (on-line or off-line). This is the library you won't outgrow. Books can be on different drives or even multiple CD-ROM drives.

■ **Full Hypertext Capability:** Electronic book texts are nearly alive with scripture references, abbreviations, illustrations, charts, diagrams, "see" and "see also" links, as well as multimedia links.

■ **Multimedia Support:** NEBRL offers full support for on-screen video, animation, and stereo sound.

■ **Multilingual Environment:** NEBRL supports Unicode and therefore is one of the first truly multilingual text searching engines, capable of displaying and implementing hypertext in dozens of known languages, ancient and modern. Both eastern and western languages as well as left-to-right and right-to-left languages have built-in support for searching and display. Search for a right-to-left Hebrew phrase embedded in a left-to-right German sentence within an English paragraph. Language can be one of the search parameters. Type or click-and-drag foreign words into your notes using the NEBRL multilingual note-taking system.

■ **Unique Word Lists for Each Language Group:** As books are added or deleted to your electronic library, NEBRL maintains unique word lists for your entire collection according to language groups. This is vitally important when used as a spelling check on search entries and it is also invaluable for discovering alternate spellings for the same words to ensure thorough research.

■ **Topic Lists for Each Book:** As books are added or deleted to your electronic library, NEBRL maintains topic lists for each book in your collection. These individual lists enable you to select from a book's topic list to access an appropriate article in the book, or NEBRL will instantly combine all of the lists from every book in your library to create a Global Topic List. This list from all of the books in your collection can then be used to access the appropriate articles which refer to a particular topic.

- **Greek and Hebrew Lemmas:** NEBRL provides embedded cross-reference numbers for Greek and Hebrew lemmas. NEBRL supports both Strong's and GK numbering schemes.

- **Versification Anomalies:** NEBRL provides support for versification anomalies. Line up the parallel text, not the parallel verse numbers.

- **Advanced Powerful Search Engine:** NEBRL offers one of the most powerful full text search engines in the electronic book world:

  In addition to pre-defined search ranges that include a single category, book, chapter, or range of verses, specify and store user-defined ranges—even noncontiguous ranges in the same book.

  Recall previous searches, edit them, and re-run the search.

  Perform searches with more than twenty search operators that allow almost any conceivable combination of searches.

  Perform reference searches which allow you to specify a Bible verse and look for every occurrence of that reference in the entire library.

  Perform filter searches which are searches restricted to the text of Bible verses referenced in a non-Bible book article.

  Use all popular wild card expressions as well as character class expressions which allow searching for a particular range of characters in a selected character position.

  Perform morphological searches, which allow searching for any part of speech in the Hebrew Old Testament, Greek New Testament, and Septuagint. Coupled with the boolean, wild card, and character class functions, extraordinary searches on grammatical constructions are possible.

  Combine multiple search methods (concordance, phrase, key word, and filter searches).

  Match words in your search queries to words in NEBRL Global Word Index, a master list of words and topics existent in the current books being searched, including foreign languages.

  Perform multilingual searches, including Greek and Hebrew (right-to-left typing for Hebrew). To search for Greek and Hebrew, the accents, breathing, and vowel points are not required.

  Search the Apocrypha (NRSV and NAB).

■ **Viewing Search Results:** You can simultaneously display search results in context from all searched books. You can transfer all or selected search results to a user note file. You can view search results highlighted in context in any document window, and you can print search results.

■ **Link Document Windows:** Link document windows for simultaneous scrolling and viewing of parallel or related passages in multiple books. Link windows selectively while leaving others independent. Link windows into separate groups, each group independent of the others.

■ **Annotations:** Attach free-form, multilingual and multimedia notes, to any article or word in any text using the exclusive NEBRL scholar's note-taking system. These notes can contain cross-references and topical indices, all unrestricted as to size, and can be stored in multiple note files.

■ **User-customizable Toolbar:** NEBRL works the way you do. Customize the Toolbar, reducing your most common tasks to a single button on the Toolbar. Toggle the Toolbar on and off.

■ **Macro Language:** For even more demanding "power users," reduce complex multiple procedures to a single user-defined button.

■ **Multi-user Configurability:** Whether multiple users work with the program or whether a single person uses the program for multiple purposes, NEBRL provides totally independent workspace environments which can be called up by file name.

■ **Common Interface for all Book Types:** Over the course of two thousand years books have changed in appearance and organization. Even today, a dictionary is organized differently than a commentary. Learn only one search system that spans your entire library regardless of type of book and publishing format.

■ **Word Processor Support:** Send Bible passages to standard word processors using the unique DVI, the most efficient transfer process ever.

■ **Bibliographic Citations:** For formal documentation, export to your word processor full bibliographic citations for the current book in user-selectable formats.

■ **Print and Export:** Print or export data from any book. Print in 1-column, 2-column, 3-column, or unformatted page formats. Export in plain ASCII text or Rich Text Format.

■ **On-line User's Guide:** The *User's Guide* itself is one of the books in the library system. Search it for information just as you would any other book.

■ **Tools for English Bible Students and Greek/Hebrew Scholars:** NEBRL is designed to take the student as far as possible. Strong's Numbers and associated lexicons based on Thayer's and Brown, Driver, Briggs allow every student the opportunity to examine the underlying Greek and Hebrew texts. More advanced students may examine the actual Greek text by clicking on English words in the New American Standard Bible which is programmed to link with the Greek text in parallel (books available from Logos). Click on the Greek word and initiate a search through several Greek lexicons available. For the original language scholars there are full morphological texts in which every word's part of speech is defined.

Latest Features of LLS in NEBRL

Library Browser

The Library Browser opens on the left side of your screen. This is one of the major new features of NEBRL. It contains a complete index or "catalog" of your entire library, organized by categories. You can use the Browser to examine the contents of all available books, open them in NEBRL, and initiate searches—among other things. Basic features and functions of the Browser are:

- Hierarchical listing of books (by category and subcategories).
- Multilingual display of book contents and major subheadings.
- Push-pin button keeps it open or auto-closes it after selection.
- Drag and drop books to the NEBRL desktop. (See **Drag and Drop Features** later in this chapter.)
- Keyboard browse control. (LEFT ARROW collapses browser levels, RIGHT ARROW expands, ENTER opens books.)
- Right mouse menu control for browse and search functions.

For details on the Library Browser, see **Library Browser**.

Toolbar

The toolbar for NEBRL is customizable. A default toolbar is provided that includes the most common functions for NEBRL. Create as many toolbars as you like, and switch between them by right-clicking on the toolbar and selecting one from the list. To edit or add toolbar buttons, go into **Preferences**, and click the **Toolbar** tab.

Linking Books

Any book can be linked to any other book(s).

For details on linking books, see **Linking Books**.

Changing the Text Size

You can change the text display size for any individual book.

For details on changing the text display sizes, see **Altering a Book's Display.**

Extra Information

In books like the KJV, you will often see an *asterisk* (*) appear above the mouse pointer. This indicates that you can get more information about the word the mouse pointer is currently over. Open the right mouse menu by clicking and holding the right mouse button, and select *Information.* A window will appear that contains information related to the word like: Strong's number, lemma for Greek and Hebrew, parsing, etc. This window can either be a floating or regular popup. A floating popup window will stay open and on top of other windows. A regular popup window will only remain until you click the mouse or begin typing on the keyboard. You can customize NEBRL to use one or the other by selecting **Preferences** from the **Edit** menu, then selecting the **General** tab.

KeyLinks

KeyLinks allow you to "link" any language to your favorite reference work for instant access. Once a KeyLink is set, you can right-click on any word and select *KeyLink* to look up that word in your keylinked reference. If the word exists, the reference will open to the matching article. Since KeyLinks are language based, you can set one for English, one for German, one for Greek, and even one for Strong's numbers. (NEBRL treats Greek Strong's, Hebrew Strong's, TVM numbers, and both Greek and Hebrew morphology as unique languages.) For example, when you right-click on English words and select KeyLink, NEBRL can automatically search the Bible dictionary of your choice, and when you right-click on Greek words, NEBRL can search your selected Greek lexicon.

Pre-set KeyLinks

NEBRL provides the following pre-set Keylinks:

- Greek Strong's Numbers: *Enhanced Strong's Lexicon*
- Hebrew Strong's Numbers: *Enhanced Strong's Lexicon*
- TVM Numbers: Tense Voice Mood book
- English: *New Nave's Topical Bible*
- Greek: Bauer, Arndt, Gingrich, and Danker *Greek Lexicon* (book available from Logos)

For details on setting and using KeyLinks, see **Languages** and **KeyLink Search.**

Drag and Drop Features

Drag and drop refers to moving information (text, pictures, files, etc.) using your mouse. To drag and drop, click and hold the left mouse button on the source data, and while holding the button down move or "drag" the data to the destination. Then release the left mouse button to "drop" the data. Try dragging and dropping information throughout the program. Examples of drag-drop areas are:

■ Library Browser to Workspace (NEBRL main window).

■ Library Browser to Search Dialog (Search Range, Books List).

■ Search Dialog, Operators List to Search Command box.

■ Any Highlighted Text to Note Field or word processor (i.e., Word 6.0).

■ Note to another note file.

■ Search result reference to note window as note label or cross reference.

Saving Your Workspace

You can save your workspace. The NEBRL workspace is defined as your arrangement of books, notes, and search results on the screen.

For details on saving your workspace, see **Preferences, General**, in Chapter Seven, "System Management."

Unlocking Titles

NEBRL provides a facility for users to shop at home and have instant access to new books after reviewing their tables of contents. These books reside on CDs from which they can be unlocked over the phone should the user choose to purchase them.

To unlock a book, see **Unlocking Titles**.

IntelliMouse Support

NEBRL supports the Microsoft IntelliMouse on Windows 95. Placing the mouse cursor over a window and rolling the wheel will cause the window to scroll, even when you are in a dialog. Clicking the mouse wheel in a window turns on auto-scroll mode. The mouse cursor will change into a multi-directional cursor, indicating the directions in which you may now scroll. Moving the mouse in one of those directions causes the window to scroll in that direction. Clicking the mouse wheel again turns off auto-scroll mode.

Orders

To order products from Nelson Electronic Publishing Direct, call the toll-free number listed in the front of this *Guide*. International Customers: The appropriate number for your country can be found at the beginning of this *Guide*.

Jumps to Internet Sites and Windows 3.1x

A hyper-text link to Nelson's World Wide Web page is available from within NEBRL. Select the Help menu option "Go To http://www.NelsonWordDirect.com". For this to work when running NEBRL on Windows 3.1x, the Internet browsing application must already be running in the background.

About This User's Guide

Chapter Two discusses how to install NEBRL on your computer and introduces you to the basic elements, such as the screen environment, keyboard shortcuts, etc.

> **NOTE:** If you are new to Windows, learn how to navigate in Windows before you continue with NEBRL, as this manual is not intended to teach the basics of using Windows. We assume you are already familiar with standard Windows techniques, menus, and use of a mouse.

Chapters Three through Five guide you through basic features of NEBRL. The study will begin with reading text and will gradually progress to demonstrating many of the tools and texts included. This *User's Guide* is meant to be worked through in front of your computer with you actually trying out each feature. Along the way you will learn (among other things) how to:

- Open and read various Bible translations, both individually and in parallel.

- View quickly any passage of the Bible, given its book name, chapter number, and starting verse number.

- View related passages of the Bible, given a set of cross-references like those in many study Bibles.

- Find articles, pictures, and maps in supplementary books, either by name or from a mention within the Bible.

- Perform searches through any number of Bibles and/or other books in your library.

- Create your own notes and cross-references in order to preserve the results of your research.

Chapter Six explains how to print and export the results of your studies. NEBRL provides full support for printing text and graphics, and for exporting text to ASCII, RTF, and HTML files and graphics to bitmap (BMP) and Windows metafiles (WMF). You will learn how to include material from your NEBRL studies in your favorite word processor documents. You will also learn how to import notes from other programs into NEBRL's advanced scholar's notes system.

You can customize the way NEBRL operates in your environment. Chapter Seven describes how to set up NEBRL according to your own personal preferences including creating your own custom Toolbar. It also details other system management functions such as unlocking books, and backing up and restoring system settings.

For those interested in Greek and/or Hebrew, Chapter Eight will extend the study using the Greek and Hebrew language tools available in NEBRL. That chapter will also be useful for those who know little or no Greek and Hebrew. NEBRL's ability to access Greek and Hebrew study tools even from an English translation expands the range of study tools available. In that chapter you will explore how to:

- View the Greek and Hebrew text, alone or with accompanying translation.

- Find the Greek or Hebrew word from which any English word was translated.

- Obtain grammatical information, such as part of speech, lemma, and brief definitions, for particular Greek and Hebrew words.

- View and use the Greek and Hebrew lexicons.

- Search the Greek and Hebrew texts in a variety of ways.

- Intermix multiple languages (including Greek and Hebrew) into one search request.

- Perform morphological searches.

Appendices are included which provide supplemental information.

Help! (Technical Support)

Thomas Nelson Publishers provides to all registered users free technical support *on the currently shipping product version*. To receive the full benefit of using The NEBRL, please fill out the enclosed registration card and mail it to Thomas Nelson.

You may reach Nelson Electronic Publishing's Technical Support Department by doing any of the following:

- Call the appropriate Technical Support voice phone number (see **Thomas Nelson Headquarters and Distributors** at the beginning of this *User's Guide*).

■ Communicate via Internet at **NelsonCDTech@ThomasNelson.com.**

When calling on our tech support voice line, please have your complete system information on hand for the technician. This would include your computer's processor type (386, 486, Pentium, etc.), your version numbers for Windows and DOS (we fully support the currently shipping Microsoft operating systems), the number of megabytes of RAM installed, and whether you are currently running a permanent swap file. We will take whatever time is necessary to answer your questions, but there are a few things we ask you to do before you contact us.

■ Please check this *User's Guide* and the README file supplied with the software for possible solutions.

■ Be sure that you can duplicate the problem repeatedly.

■ Remove unnecessary TSRs (Terminate and Stay Resident programs) from your config.sys file and close any other open Windows and DOS applications, then reopen NEBRL, checking to see if the problem still occurs.

Tip of the Day

When you start NEBRL, the **Tip of the Day** dialog will appear to give you a quick "how-to" suggestion on using NEBRL. To see more than one tip, click *Next Tip*.

If you do not want to see the tip, click the Show Tip on Startup box in the lower left corner of the dialog to deselect it. The tips will no longer appear.

To make the tips reappear:

1. Select *Tip of the Day* from the **Help** menu (ALT+H,D).

2. Click the Show Tip on Startup box in the dialog to select it. Click *Close*.

2

Getting Started

In this section we will walk you through the installation and starting procedures for *Nelson's Electronic Bible Reference Library* (NEBRL). We will also explain the various NEBRL screen elements, buttons, available on-screen Help, and keyboard shortcuts.

System Requirements

The system requirements for running The NEBRL are:

- Any Microsoft Windows 3.1, or later, compatible system (minimum of 486sx, DOS 3.3).

- 8Mb of RAM memory required, 16Mb or more recommended.

- Any Microsoft Windows 3.1, or later, compatible VGA graphics card and monitor.

- Hard disk with at least 15 megabytes free.

- Double-speed or better CD-ROM drive.

How Do I Install NEBRL?

1. Insert the NEBRL CD-ROM you purchased: *Starter Edition* CD, or *Basic Edition* CD#1, or *Deluxe Edition* CD#1 in your CD-ROM drive.

2. If you are running **Windows 3.1**, select File . . . Run in the Program Manager. If you are running **Windows 95**, select Start . . . Run, or if you have Autoplay enabled, the Setup will automatically run.

3. In the Run dialog's Command: line (**for Windows 3.1**) or Open: line (**for Windows 95**), type D:\SETUP (Where D: is your CD-ROM drive letter).

4. Click "OK". Follow the on-screen instructions to complete setup.

Setup Complete! When this message appears, you are ready to start NEBRL.

How Do I Get Free Tech Support and Other Benefits? The Nelson Electronic Advantage program

Fill out and mail the Registration Card today, which automatically enrolls you in the Nelson Electronic Advantage program. It is very important that you complete and return your registration, so that you will be eligible for free technical support, special discounts on unlocking books, and product upgrade announcements. Owners of the *Starter Edition:* call the toll-free number to register.

What About This CD#2 in My Basic or Deluxe Edition?

The *Basic* and *Deluxe Editions* include a second CD-ROM with additional books which may be unlocked. It is not necessary to install CD#2 to use the books you purchased in the *Basic* and *Deluxe Editions.* However, you will want to also view CD#2 at your earliest convenience to browse the list of valuable titles instantly available to you. To view this CD-ROM (or other LLS collections available from other publishers which you may own or purchase), start NEBRL with CD#1 in your CD-ROM drive, and select Restart with New CD from the drop-down File menu at the top of your screen. Insert CD#2 in your CD-ROM drive, and click OK. For instructions on how to unlock additional books, see the section near the back of this *Guide.* Owners of the *Starter Edition* can exchange it with their local Christian retailer for a $10 discount off the regular retail price of the *Basic* or *Deluxe Edition,* or they can call the toll-free number listed on the back of the CD-ROM case to request a copy of CD#2 or purchase the *Basic* or *Deluxe Editions.* (The *Starter Edition* trade-in program is only valid with participating local retailers.)

Problems Installing NEBRL?

If you have experienced problems installing NEBRL, please print the SETUP.LOG file which is in your LOGOS20 directory from Windows Write or other word processor (not Notepad). This contains information about the installation process including when the problem occurred. Please have this information available when you contact Nelson's Tech Support. For information on contacting Tech Support see **Help** in Chapter One.

Starting NEBRL

Windows 95™

—From the Desktop

NEBRL runs well in both Win 95 and Win 3.1. You can run NEBRL from the Win 95 desktop just like any other Win 95 compatible program.

—From the Start *Button*

If your installation of Logos was successful, you should have a new program group on your Start Menu. Click the Start button (lower left-hand corner of your screen, typically); on the menu that pops up, choose Programs → Nelson Electronic Library, and finally, Nelson Electronic Library.

—From My Computer

Double-click on the My Computer icon on your desktop. Depending on how your machine is configured, you'll have a number of available drives. Choose the hard disk drive where you've installed the Logos Library System and double-click on it. There should be a folder on that drive named Logos20. Double-click on it. The Nelson Electronic Library program file resides in that folder, under the name of Logos.exe. Double-click on it, and you're in.

Windows 3.1™

—From the Program Manager

Open the Program Manager by double-clicking on its icon (if not open already), and then double-click on the Nelson's Electronic Library program group. Double-click on the Nelson Electronic Library icon, and away you go.

Start-up Splash Screen

The Logos Library System, on which *Nelson's Electronic Bible Reference Library* is built, is an *integrated library, notes editor, and text retrieval-search viewer.* The key word here is "library." When you start NEBRL, not only must the software viewer load, but the librarian must also scan your library, locating and identifying all of your books. The result is that the NEBRL main screen cannot appear until the librarian has identified all books, because part of the main screen is the Library Browser's list of books currently available for search and retrieval. Therefore, the total startup time for NEBRL is dependent on the number of books in your library. When all of your books have been identified, the main screen will appear and you may begin your work.

Problems Starting NEBRL?

Windows 3.1

If you are experiencing problems starting NEBRL, start NEBRL by running *LOGOS /B* from File Run as follows:

1. From Program Manager, select the File menu.

2. From the File menu, select Run.

3. In the Run Command Line, type *C:\LOGOS20\LOGOS.EXE /B* and click OK. After the error occurs, print C:\LOGOS20\BOOTLOG.LOG from Windows Write or other word processor (not Notepad). Please have this information available when you contact Thomas Nelson Tech Support. For information on contacting Tech Support see **Help** in chapter one.

Windows 95

If you are experiencing problems starting NEBRL while running Windows 95, start NEBRL from a Run command as follows:

1. Click on Start and then on Run.

2. On the Open line, type in *C:\LOGOS20\LOGOS.EXE /B* and then click OK. After the error, find the file BOOTLOG.LOG in the LOGOS20 directory and double click on it. Take it to Writepad, and print it out. Please have this information available when you contact Thomas Nelson Tech Support. For information on contacting Tech Support see **Help** in chapter one.

The NEBRL/Windows Environment

You should feel comfortable with the screen environment of Nelson's Electronic Bible Reference Library. The look and feel is thoroughly Windows. Following we have listed the many elements of the NEBRL screen, with the list keyed to the NEBRL/Windows screen environment (Fig. 2-1).

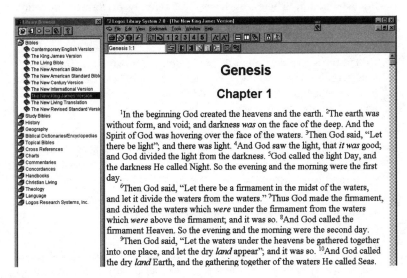

Figure 2-1 NEBRL/Windows Screen Environment.

1. **Title Bar.** The Title Bar displays the name of the book or user note file that is open in the active window.

2. **Minimize.** Clicking this button reduces the NEBRL screen to an icon on your taskbar with the program remaining active. Click on the icon to restore NEBRL to its original screen size.

3. **Maximize.** With NEBRL smaller than full screen size, clicking this button will enlarge NEBRL to fill the screen. With NEBRL maximized, this button changes to the **Restore** button (up and down arrow). Clicking the Restore button returns NEBRL to its original size.

4. **Close Button.** This button closes NEBRL.

5. **Menu Bar.** The Menu Bar displays the names of the pull-down menus from which NEBRL features can be accessed.

6. **Toolbar.** The Toolbar displays "Buttons," shortcuts to specific program functions. (See **Toolbar**, later in this chapter.)

7. **Window Title Bar.** Displays the title of the window's book.

8. **Bible Reference Box.** Displays current Scripture reference. Click in this box, type a new Bible reference, then press ENTER, to move to that verse [TAB or CTRL+G].

9. **Active Document Window.** Each book resides in its own document window. The active document window is the window with the highlighted title bar where you have most recently performed an action (e.g., scrolling, selecting text, etc.).

10. **Vertical Scroll Bar.** Clicking either the up or down button scrolls the data in the active document window. Holding down either button provides continuous scrolling. Clicking in the area between the up and down buttons rapidly jumps toward the top or bottom of the document window's data [UP ARROW, DOWN ARROW].

11. **Sliding Scroll Button.** Clicking and holding down this button while sliding it up and down moves rapidly through a document window's data. The sliding scroll button's relative position on the vertical scroll bar indicates the display's current relative position in the book. For example, if the button is one quarter of the way down from the top of the scroll bar, the display is one quarter of the way from the beginning of the book.

12. **Library Browser.** The Library Browser functions like a card catalog in a public library. Using the Browser, you can locate any book, chapter, or article in your electronic library.

13. **Status Bar.** Displays a short message describing command functions as they are accessed.

14. **Dynamic Verse Insertion (DVI) Button.** Pressing this button activates the DVI dialog for Bible verse insertion into your Windows-based word processor.

The Menu Bar

The **Menu Bar** is a horizontal menu that runs across the top of all Windows applications. Options displayed include: **File, Edit, View,** etc. Each of these options, when selected, will display a "pull-down" menu with additional options. Each of these options will be discussed later in this manual.

The Toolbar

The **Toolbar** displays a row of labeled buttons. These buttons are shortcuts to specific program functions and often replace several keystrokes or pull-down menu selections. These "Buttons" significantly speed up the most commonly used features. You can customize the Toolbar by adding and deleting buttons. You can also create custom program functions to suit your individual requirements, storing these functions as macros and then assigning them to buttons on the Toolbar for easy access. Display of the Toolbar can be toggled on or off. (See **Preferences, Toolbar** in chapter seven, "System Management.")

The Status Bar

The **Status Bar** is an information line at the bottom of the NEBRL work space which displays status information. When a menu is open, the Status Bar displays a short message describing the action that the highlighted command performs.

Keyboard Commands

Rather than clicking with the mouse on the Menu options and pull-down menu selections, experienced users often prefer to use equivalent keyboard commands to accomplish the same task. In this *User's Guide* these keyboard commands appear in parentheses. For example, (ALT+F,X) is the same as clicking on the **File Menu**, then choosing *Exit*, to exit NEBRL.

Keyboard Shortcuts

Most NEBRL features can be accessed from the Toolbar as noted above or from the Menu Bar either by mouse or by holding down the ALT key and hitting the underlined letter of the menu option desired (Keyboard Commands). However, there are also a number of keyboard shortcuts designed to help experienced users get around quickly. These keyboard shortcuts will appear inside brackets after the standard keyboard commands which occur in parentheses. For example: (ALT+F,X) [CTRL+Q].

Right Mouse Functions

Many NEBRL features can be accessed from right mouse menus which are available by clicking the *right* mouse button anywhere in the program. Functions which can be accessed from a right mouse menu will appear in this *User's Guide* inside parentheses. For example, (+D) indicates Right Mouse menu, *Define KeyLink*.

So, anywhere in the program, if in doubt, *try clicking the right mouse button.* You will often discover a right mouse function to speed you along. For example, while there are a number of different ways to open a book in NEBRL, by far the fastest way is simply to right-click on a book title in the Library Browser, then click *View Selection* on the right- mouse menu.

Using Help

You can enter Help in a number of different ways:

■ Choose *Index* from the **Help Menu** and you will be given a menu of instruction topics on how to use NEBRL (ALT+H,I) [F1].

■ Click the **Help** button found on the Toolbar.

■ Click the *right* mouse button. Choose *Help* from the right mouse menu.

■ When in a dialog box, click the *Help* button for context-sensitive help anywhere inside NEBRL.

Exit Help in one of the following ways:

- Choose **File** from the Help Menu Bar and then choose *Exit* (ALT+F,X).
- Choose the Help **Control Menu** (–) and then choose *Close* (ALT+SPACE,C).
- Double-click on the Help **Control Menu** (–).

3

Viewing a Book

Library Browser: Pulling a Book off the Library Shelf

Point and Click Book Selection

We will focus on selecting a Bible passage, Exodus 12:37–51, the exodus of the children of Israel from Egypt in the KJV Bible. There are numerous ways to pull the KJV Bible off the library shelf and open it to Exodus 12:37–51 utilizing the hierarchical structure of the Library Browser. These methods apply to opening any type of book. In addition, the main Toolbar can be customized to provide a New Bible Window button which can be used as a quick way to open Bibles only.

When you enter NEBRL for the first time you see the opening screen (**Fig. 2-1**). The screen is divided into two windows: the large work space on the right and the Library Browser on the left. The **Library Browser** is a catalog system which enables you to quickly locate a book and pull it off the shelf for reading.

To select a book:

1. **Select a book category.** Initially the Browser displays the list of categories into which your book collection has been divided (Antiquities, History, Dictionaries, Encyclopedias, etc.). In the future, as you purchase new books, this list of categories will grow to match the categories of new books. When you first open NEBRL, the Browser will display all categories, subcategories, and the book titles within the categories (Fig. 2-1). When the categories are collapsed so that the book titles are hidden (Fig. 3-1), you can open a category (in this case, "Bibles") (Fig. 3-2), by doing any of the following:

   ■ Click the mouse on the category "Bibles" to highlight it, and then click the **Expand** button on the Browser Toolbar (⌘+E). The Bibles category will expand, displaying the titles of all available Bibles.

   ■ Click the mouse on the category "Bibles" to highlight it, and then click the **Show Books** button on the Browser Toolbar (⌘+A). All categories will expand, displaying the titles of all available books on your system.

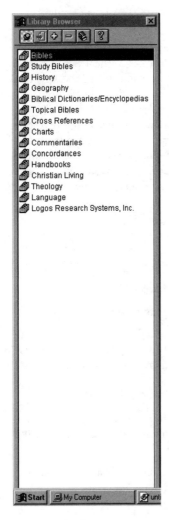

Figure 3-1 Library Browser, Collapsed Categories.

■ Click the mouse on the category icon next to the word "Bibles," or double-click on the word "Bibles." The Bibles category will expand, displaying the titles of all available Bibles.

■ Click the mouse anywhere within the Browser window, causing the Browser to become the active window. Press the keyboard DOWN AR-ROW, highlighting each category as you move down the list. Stop when the desired category is highlighted. To expand the Bibles category, after you have experimented moving the highlight bar down the list, return to "Bibles" (using the UP ARROW), high-lighting it. Press the keyboard RIGHT ARROW. The Bibles category will ex-pand, displaying the titles of all available Bibles.

2. **Select a book from the appropriate category.** To select the KJV, do one of the following:

■ Click the KJV to highlight it. Click the **Expand** button ![Expand button] on the Browser Toolbar, causing it to display the list of Bible books (e.g., Genesis, Exodus, etc.) (⌥+E) (Fig. 3-3).

■ Click the mouse on the book icon next to the words "The King James Version," or double-click on the words "The King James Version" causing it to display the list of Bible books.

■ Using the keyboard DOWN ARROW, move the highlight bar down the list of Bibles until the KJV is highlighted. Press the keyboard RIGHT AR-ROW, causing it to display the list of Bible books.

3. **Select and display the desired passage in the book.** In our example we want to view Exodus 12:37–51. First, select the book of Exodus. Scroll down the list of Bible books using either the keyboard DOWN ARROW or

Figure 3-2 The Bible Category Expanded.

clicking the mouse on the Down Arrow at the bottom of the Browser Vertical Scroll Bar. To scroll down the list rapidly, use the keyboard PAGE DOWN or click and drag the Sliding Scroll Button down the Vertical Scroll Bar until Exodus appears in view. Use any of the preceding methods to expand Exodus and display the list of chapters (⌐+E). Follow the same procedure to scroll down to chapter 12. To view chapter 12, do one of the following:

■ Click chapter 12 to highlight it. Click the **View Selection** button

 on the Browser Toolbar (⌐+V).

■ Double-click chapter 12.

■ Click chapter 12 to highlight it. Press ENTER.

A "document window" will open in the main work space with the title "King James Version" in the Title Bar, displaying Exodus 12 (Fig. 3-4).

Drag and Drop Book Selection

To drag a book from the Library Browser and drop it into the main work space, causing it to open in a document window:

1. Select a book, chapter, or article to open by highlighting it in the Browser.

2. Click the highlighted item with the left mouse button and, while holding down the button, drag the item to the right into the main work space.

3. When the cursor changes to the book cursor 📖 , release the left mouse button and the selected item will open in a document window.

New Bible Window

The New Bible Window function enables you to quickly open a Bible window to Genesis 1:1 without using the Browser. Access New Bible Window using either of the following methods:

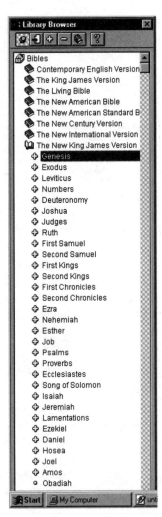

Figure 3-3 Book Expanded, Chapters Displayed.

■ Click the New Bible Window button on the main Toolbar. NEBRL will check to see if your "preferred" Bible is open. (See **Preferred Bible** in chapter seven, "System Management.") If it is not, NEBRL will open it. If it is already open, NEBRL will open (in alphabetical order) the first closed Bible from your Bible list in the Library Browser. (To use the New Bible Window button, you must first customize the main Toolbar so that it includes this button. See **Toolbar** in chapter seven, "System Management.")

■ Select *New Bible Window* from the **Window** menu (ALT+W,N) [F5].

New Bible and Reference

The New Bible and Reference function enables you to quickly open a Bible window *to any desired reference* without using the Browser. Access New Bible and Reference using either of the following methods:

■ Click the New Bible Window button on the main Toolbar *while holding down the CTRL key*. NEBRL will open the **New Bible Window** dialog. Select the Bible version to be opened and the reference to which it should be opened. Click *OK* to open the Bible to the desired reference. (To use the New Bible Window button, you must first customize the main Toolbar so that it includes this button. See **Toolbar** in chapter seven, "System Management.")

■ Select *New Bible and Reference* from the **Window** menu to access the New Bible Window dialog (ALT+W,B) [CTRL+F5].

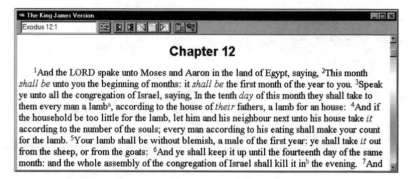

Figure 3-4 Document Window Displaying Exodus 12, KJV.

Opening Multiple Books

NEBRL enables you to open multiple different books, each in its own window (e.g., two different Bibles, a commentary, and a Bible dictionary). You can also open multiple copies of the same book in different windows.

Opening Multiple Books: Drag and Drop

When dragging a book title from the Browser to the main work space, there are two possibilities:

- You can drag the book title into a document window which already exists (Fig. 3-5, #1). The book open cursor will appear as in the illustration. NEBRL will open the book in the selected window, closing the book which had previously occupied the window.

- You can drag the book title into the main work space outside of any current document windows (Fig. 3-5, #2). In this case, NEBRL will always open a new document window for the book. This is true even if you already have the book open in another document window.

Example: If you already have the KJV Bible open and you drag it from the Browser into the main work space *but not within any currently open windows,* NEBRL will open a second copy of the KJV. You can use these two copies of the KJV independently of one another, just as if you had two separate copies of this Bible sitting on your desk.

Opening Multiple Books: Control Key

When opening a book, regardless of whether you use drag and drop, right mouse menus, or the keyboard, if you *hold down the* CTRL *key* while you open the book, NEBRL will always open the book in a new window.

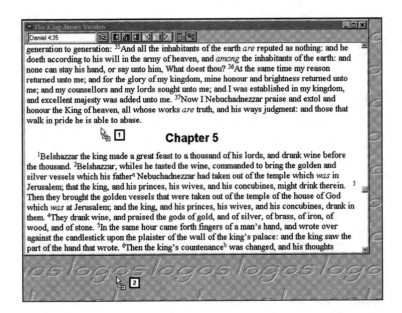

Figure 3-5 Book Open Cursor in Document Window (1). Book Open Cursor in Main Work Space (2).

Example: Dragging a book title onto an already-open window normally replaces the book with the new book in the same window. However, if you are holding down the CTRL key while you drag the book onto the window, NEBRL will open a new window, leaving the other book still open. Notice that when holding down the CTRL key during drag and drop, the book

open cursor has a plus sign (+) attached ![cursor icon] , indicating a new window will be created.

In the same way, if you open books with the **View Selection** button

![button icon] on the Browser Toolbar, you can open multiple copies of the same book by holding down the CTRL key while you click View Selection.

Opening Non-Bible Books

Opening non-Bible books is virtually the same as opening Bibles with but a few exceptions. One exception is that the **New Bible Window** button

![button icon] on the Toolbar opens only Bibles, so that all non-Bibles must be opened from the Library Browser. All non-Bibles can be divided into two

types of books: versified and nonversified. While some books could be arranged in a biblical verse order, generally only Bible commentaries follow this scheme. Nonversified books are arranged by chapters and/or articles. Many sections of these nonversified books can also be identified by key topics.

Opening Versified Non-Bible Books

To open versified non-Bibles (e.g., Bible commentaries), do the following:

1. From the Library Browser open the category "Commentaries" by: (1) clicking the category icon; or (2) double-clicking the word "Commen-

   taries"; or (3) clicking "Categories" and then the Expand button or pressing the keyboard RIGHT ARROW.

NOTE: You will have the category "Commentaries" listed in your Library Browser only if you have purchased a Bible commentary such as *Matthew Henry's Commentary* or *Harper's Bible Commentary*. If you do not have Commentaries in the library, skip this section and move on to "Opening Nonversified Books."

2. Using either the keyboard DOWN ARROW or the mouse, highlight the commentary you want to open.

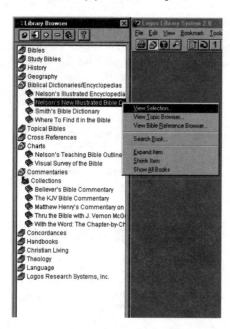

Figure 3-6 View Selection From the Right Mouse Menu.

3. You have various choices:

■ Open the commentary's table of contents by: (1) clicking the book icon; or (2) double-clicking its title; or (3) with the title highlighted, pressing the keyboard RIGHT ARROW. Using the keyboard DOWN ARROW or the mouse cursor, move the highlight bar down the hierarchical list of the commentary's table of contents until you have positioned the highlight bar on the section which discusses the desired Bible book and chapter. (1) Double-click on the desired section of the commentary, much as you would open a Bible; or (2) click the **View Selection** button on the Browser Toolbar; or (3) click *View Selection* on the right mouse menu (Fig. 3-6) (☝+V).

■ With the highlight bar on the name of the commentary, click *View Bible Reference Browser* on the right mouse menu (☝+R). The **Bible Reference Browser** will open with the commentary selected for reference search (Fig. 3-7). In the Search For box, enter a Bible reference. A list of matching articles will appear in the Articles list box. Select the

desired article and click the *View Selection* button .

Figure 3-7 Bible Reference Browser.

■ Drag the commentary into the main work space. Select the *Bible Reference Browser* from the **View Menu** (ALT+V,R) [CTRL+R]. Proceed as in the previous method.

■ Drag the commentary title into the main work space. When it opens in a window, press CTRL+G or TAB to position the cursor in the Bible Reference Box ready for your input. For example, enter:

Exodus 12:1 or Ex 12.1 or Ex 12

The commentary will display the section closest to your request. Versified books display in windows with a Bible Reference Box, therefore you can move around in them much as you would in a Bible.

■ Before you open the commentary, press CTRL+R. The **Reference Browser** will open. For a complete discussion of the Reference Browser, see **Reference Browser** in this chapter.

Opening Nonversified Books

To open nonversified books such as the *Nelson's New Illustrated Bible Dictionary,* do the following:

1. In the Library Browser open the category "Dictionaries" by: (1) clicking the category icon; or (2) double-clicking the word "Dictionaries"; or (3)

clicking "Dictionaries" followed by the Expand button or pressing the keyboard RIGHT ARROW.

2. Using either the keyboard DOWN ARROW or the mouse, highlight the *Nelson's New Illustrated Bible Dictionary.*

3. You have various choices:

■ Open the dictionary's table of contents by: (1) clicking the book icon; or (2) double-clicking its title; or (3) clicking the title and then clicking

the Expand button [image] or pressing the keyboard RIGHT ARROW. Using the keyboard DOWN ARROW or the mouse cursor, move the highlight bar down the hierarchical list of the dictionary's table of contents until you have positioned the highlight bar on the desired topic. (1) Double-click on the topic; or (2) click the **View Selection** button

[image] on the Browser Toolbar; or (3) click *View Selection* on the right mouse menu (⌐+V).

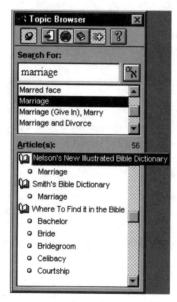

Figure 3-8 Topic Browser.

■ With the *Nelson's New Illustrated Bible Dictionary* highlighted, click *View Topic Browser* on the right mouse menu (⌐+T). The **Topic Browser** will open with the *Nelson's New Illustrated Bible Dictionary* selected for topic search (Fig. 3-8). In the Search For box, enter a topic; or from the list, scroll down and click a topic. A list of matching articles will appear in the Articles list box. Select the desired article and click

the *View Selection* button [image] or double-click the article title.

■ Click the **Topic Browser** button

[image] on the main Toolbar. Proceed as in the previous method.

■ Drag the dictionary title into the main work space. Select *Topic Browser* from the **View** menu (ALT+V,K) [CTRL+K]. Proceed as in the previous method.

■ Drag the dictionary title into the main work space. Select the *Bible Reference Browser* from the **View Menu** (ALT+V,R) [CTRL+R]. Enter or select a Bible reference. A list of matching articles will appear in the Articles list box. Select the desired article and click the *View Selection*

button .

- Before you open the dictionary, press CTRL+K. The **Topic Browser** will open. For a complete discussion of the Topic Browser, see **Topic Browser** in this chapter.

Icons, Pluses, Minuses, and Bullets

The following symbols are used in the Library Browser:

- **Icons.** Categories, subcategories, and individual books use icons depicting a card index, a shelf of books, and a single book, respectively. These icons indicate that the item contains further subdivisions. For example, when you open the category "Bibles," the card index icon in front of Bibles changes to show a card being removed from the index. Similarly, when you open a book, the icon changes from a closed book to an open book.

- **Plus Sign** (+). The + indicates that this subdivision of the book (chapters or articles) contains further subdivisions. For example, in the Bible the book of Genesis contains a level of subdivisions called chapters. Therefore, Genesis has a Plus Sign in front of it. In some Bible versions (e.g., the NIV), the chapters are further subdivided into articles, so the chapters have Plus Signs as well. For example, Exodus 12 (NIV) is divided into articles such as: "The Passover," "The Exodus," etc.

- **Minus Sign** (–). The – indicates that this subdivision of the book is open to at least the next level of subdivisions. For example, when you open the book of Exodus, the plus sign in front of Exodus changes to a minus sign because the book is open to the next level, chapters.

- **Bullet (■).** The ■ indicates that this subdivision is the final level with no further subdivisions beneath it. In the KJV the chapters have bullets in front of them because in the KJV (unlike the NIV) the chapters are not further divided into articles. Double-clicking a final subdivision displays it for viewing in a document window.

Library Browser Toolbar

The Library Browser has its own Toolbar. It contains the following buttons:

1. **Keep Browser Open.** [icon] If selected, the Library Browser will stay open after opening a book, enabling efficient access to additional books. If you unselect this button, when you open a book the Browser will disappear.

You can also close the Browser at any time by clicking the close button in the upper corner (Windows 3.1, left corner; Windows 95, right corner). To redisplay the Browser:

■ Click the **Library Browser** button ░░ on the main Toolbar.

■ Select *Library Browser* from the **View Menu** (ALT+V,B) [CTRL+B].

If you click in the title bar "Library Browser," while holding down the left mouse button you can drag the window anywhere on the screen. Because the Browser is an information popup, whenever you recall it to the screen it will reappear where you last positioned it. (See **Popup Windows** in chapter seven, "System Management.")

2. **View Selection.** ░░ View the contents of the currently selected book, chapter, or article. With a book, chapter, or chapter article highlighted, clicking this button will open to the first page of the selection and display it in a window.

3. **Expand (Right Arrow).** ░░ Expand the selected Library Browser item. Click this button or press the keyboard right arrow to list the next level of subdivisions of the selected item. For example, if a dictionary is selected, expanding it will display the list of chapters, typically a list of the letters of the alphabet. For this button to be active (highlighted), the highlight bar must be on an item which can be opened (e.g., a category, subcategory, or book) or an item with a Plus Sign (+) in front of it (e.g., chapter or article).

4. **Shrink (Left Arrow).** ░░ Shrink the selected Library Browser item. Close the current level of subdivisions. For this button to be active (highlighted), the highlight bar must be on an item which has open subdivisions beneath it.

5. **Show Books.** ░░ Expand the Browser to display all book titles in all categories.

6. **Help.** ░░ Display Library Browser Help.

Library Browser Tool Tips

Sliding the mouse cursor over the Library Browser entries will cause the Browser Tool Tips to appear, displaying in full the titles which are wider than the width of the Browser window.

Topic Browser

Press CTRL+K. The **Topic Browser** will open (Fig. 3-8). There are a number of possibilities:

■ The Browse All Books button will be pre-selected if you do not currently have any topically-indexed books open. With this option selected, in the Search For box, enter a topic; or from the list, scroll down and click a topic. A list of matching articles from all of the topically-indexed books in your library will appear in the Articles list box. Select the

appropriate article and click the *View Selection* button ![icon] or double-click the article title.

■ Only the active book's topic list will be displayed if there is a book open which has a topic index. Select and display an appropriate article as in the previous method.

■ To choose a different book's topic list, click the Choose New Book button

![icon] on the Topic Browser Toolbar (Fig. 3-8). The **Choose Book** dialog opens. Select a book just as you would from the main Library Browser. Greyed books cannot be selected because they do not have topic indexes.

■ To display all available topics from all books in your library, click the

Browse All Books button ![icon]. If this option is already selected, unselecting it will return you to the topic list from the book most recently chosen in the current NEBRL session, or, if no individual book's list has yet been chosen, it will automatically open the **Choose Book** dialog.

■ To display all of each book's articles relating to a given topic, select the

Auto-Expand Hits button ![icon]. Unselecting this option will cause only the titles of the books containing the selected topic to be listed. To display the individual articles for one of the books in the list, double-click the book title. The Auto-Expand Hits option is always selected when you are listing the topics for a single book. Therefore, you can only unselect it when the Browse All Books button is selected.

Topic Browser Not Available Globally

If the Topic Browser cannot be opened globally or is not available when no books are open, the Global Word List is out of date and needs to be rebuilt.

To rebuild the Global Word List, open NEBRL, select the Tools menu and choose Rebuild Global Word List.

Bible Reference Browser

Press CTRL+R. The **Bible Reference Browser** will open (Fig. 3-7). There are a number of possibilities:

- The Browse All Books button ⬤ will be pre-selected if you do not currently have any books with Bible references open. With this option selected, in the Search For box, enter a Bible reference. A list of matching articles from all of the books in your library will appear in the Articles list box. Select the appropriate article and click the *View Selection* button or double-click the article title.

- Only the active book's reference list will be displayed if there is a book open which has Bible references. Select and display an appropriate article as in the previous method.

- To choose a different book's reference list, click the Choose New Book button 📖 on the Bible Reference Browser Toolbar (Fig. 3-7). The **Choose Book** dialog opens. Select a book just as you would from the main Library Browser. Greyed books cannot be selected because they do not have Bible references.

- To display all available Bible references from all books in your library, click the Browse All Books button ⬤ . If this option is already selected, unselecting it will return you to the reference list from the book most recently chosen in the current NEBRL session, or, if no individual book's list has yet been chosen, it will automatically open the **Choose Book** dialog.

- To display all of each book's articles relating to a given Bible reference, select the Auto-Expand Hits button ⊞ . Unselecting this option will cause only the titles of the books containing the selected reference to be listed. To display the individual articles for one of the books in the list, double-click the book title. The Auto-Expand Hits option is always selected when you are listing the references for a single book. Therefore, you can only unselect it when the Browse All Books button is selected.

- To cause the Bible Reference Browser to automatically browse your library for articles relating to the current verse position in your active

Bible or commentary, select the Auto-Browse button [image] on the Bible Reference Browser Toolbar. With Auto-Browse selected, as you jump from verse to verse in a Bible the Bible Reference Browser will automatically browse your library and update its display of articles relevant to your current verse position.

Choose Book Dialog

The **Choose Book Dialog** (Fig. 3-8a) can be accessed using the Choose New Book button [image] on the toolbar of the **Topic Browser** or the **Bible Reference Browser**.

Figure 3-8a Choose Book Dialog.

■ Select a book just as you would from the main Library Browser. Greyed books cannot be selected because they do not contain anything for you to browse. Click *OK* to make your newly selected book the one you are browsing.

Switching Bible Versions and Commentaries

After you have opened a Bible version in a document window, you can switch the window to a different Bible version. To switch Bible versions in the active document window:

1. Make the document window active by clicking anywhere within it. The window's title bar becomes highlighted.

2. Press either the keyboard LEFT ARROW or RIGHT ARROW to cycle respectively either up or down through the Library Browser's list of Bible versions.

Each Bible will position itself at the same relative position in the text if possible. NEBRL skips Bibles which do not contain the reference at which you are currently positioned. For example, a Bible is positioned at Daniel 4:35 and you switch Bibles by pressing the RIGHT ARROW. The next Bible in the Browser is a Greek New Testament which does not contain Daniel 4:35. NEBRL will skip the Greek New Testament and go to the next Bible in the Browser list which contains the book of Daniel.

Navigating in a Book

Once you have a book open in a window, there are a number of things you can do to navigate through the book.

Moving to a New Bible Verse

The **Bible Reference Box** in the upper left-hand corner of a versified document window (e.g., Bibles, Bible commentaries) displays the current reference. As you navigate through the Bible, this field will reflect the reference being viewed in that Bible window (Fig. 3-9).

Figure 3-9 Bible Reference Box Displaying Genesis 1:1.

You can move to a new Bible verse using either the Bible Reference Box or the Reference Navigator.

Bible Reference Box

To move to a new verse using the Bible Reference Box:

1. Select the reference in the Bible Reference Box by clicking and dragging the mouse over it [CTRL+G or TAB].

   NOTE: The phrase "click and drag the mouse" over text means to click the left mouse button on the left-most character of the text and, while holding down the button, drag the mouse pointer onto the right-most character of the text. This causes the highlight to grow with the movement of the mouse until all of the desired text is highlighted at which point you release the left mouse button.

2. Type in a new reference, then press ENTER.

   NOTE: When typing a reference you may use most conventional abbreviations, e.g., "II Chron," "2 Ch," "2nd Chron," or "Second Chronicles" for "2 Chronicles." Consult Appendix A in this *User's Guide* for a list of acceptable abbreviations.

Reference Navigator

To move to a new verse using the Reference Navigator:

■ Click the **Reference Navigator** button on the document window Toolbar [CTRL+G+G]. The **Go To Reference** dialog opens (Fig. 3-10). Select the desired book, chapter, and verse. Then click *OK*.

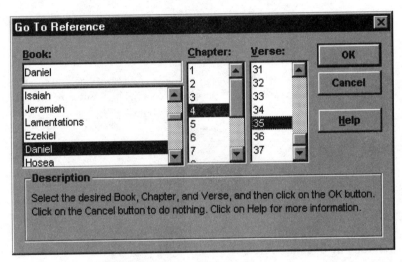

Figure 3-10 Go To Reference Dialog.

Browsing Text

To browse the text forwards or backwards in any book, use the following options:

■ Click the Up or Down Arrow of the **Vertical Scroll Bar** with the mouse to move the text forward or backward a line at a time. Clicking, and holding down, the **Sliding Scroll Button** and sliding it up or down scrolls more quickly toward the beginning or end of a book. Scrolling Tool Tips appear beside the sliding scroll button displaying your current location in the book as you scroll.

■ Use the keyboard UP ARROW and DOWN ARROW to scroll the text one line at a time. Make certain the document window has the "focus" by clicking with the mouse anywhere within it (highlighting the Title Bar). Otherwise the keyboard keys will have no effect on the window.

Sync Browser

As you browse through a book, you can sync the Library Browser to your current book location by selecting Sync Browser. Sync Browser will cause the Library Browser to display your current location by expanding the book's categories and subcategories, highlighting the article title of your current location.

To select Sync Browser:

- Click the **Sync Browser** button on the document window Toolbar.

- Select *Sync Browser* from the **View** menu (ALT+V,Y) [CTRL+Y].

Scrolling by Books (Bibles) and by Articles (Non-Bibles)

To move quickly through the Bible from the beginning of one book to the beginning of another, or through non-Bibles from the beginning of one article within a chapter to another, click the **Previous Book (Article)** or **Next Book (Article)** buttons respectively (Fig. 3-11).

Figure 3-11 Previous Book (Article), Next Book (Article).

Scrolling by Chapters (Bibles)

To move quickly through the Bible from the beginning of one chapter to the beginning of the previous/next chapter, do one of the following:

- Click the **Previous Chapter** or **Next Chapter** buttons respectively (Fig. 3-12).

Figure 3-12 Previous Chapter, Reference Navigator, Next Chapter.

- Press the keyboard SHIFT+PGUP and SHIFT+PGDN.

Scrolling One Window-full at a Time

To scroll through the text one window-full at a time, do one of the following:

- Click above or below the Sliding Scroll Button on the Vertical Scroll Bar, that is, in the area between the button and the up and down arrows on the scroll bar.

- Press the keyboard PGUP and PGDN.

Jumping to Distant Chapters and Articles

Using the Bible as an example, rather than scrolling through one Bible book after another to get to Isaiah from Genesis, you can jump to distant Bible books, chapters, and articles:

- If the book is versified (e.g., Bibles, Bible commentaries), the document window contains a Bible Reference Box. To go to the first chapter of Isaiah, click in the Bible Reference Box [CTRL+G], then type:

    Is

Press ENTER. The Bible window jumps to the beginning of Isaiah.

To go to the beginning of the twelfth chapter of Exodus, click in the Bible Reference Box [CTRL+G], then type:

    Ex 12

Press ENTER. The Bible window jumps to the beginning of chapter 12.

- If the book is versified (e.g., Bibles, Bible commentaries), click the **Reference Navigator** button on the document window Toolbar [CTRL+G+G]. The **Go To Reference** dialog opens (Fig. 3-10). Select the desired book, chapter, and verse. Then click *OK*.

- To jump to distant locations in non-Bibles, keep the Browser on the screen or redisplay it by clicking the **Library Browser** button on the main Toolbar [CTRL+B]. Expand the book in the Browser to display the chapter and/or article list. Double-click the desired chapter or article, or click the **View Selection** button, or press the ENTER key (⌘+V).

Bible Target Window

A versified book window (e.g., Bible, Bible commentary) can be designated as the "Bible Target Window." Designating a window as the Bible Target Window, selects that Bible (or commentary) as the Bible to be used when you click Ref Marks in other books. (See **Hot Spots** elsewhere in this chapter.)

To designate a window as the Bible Target Window, do either of the following:

- Click the **Bible Target Window** button on the target window's Toolbar.

■ Click anywhere inside the target window, highlighting its title bar and making it the active window. Select *Bible Target Window* from the **View** menu (ALT+V,G).

Example: You have three different Bibles open, the KJV, NKJV, and the NIV. You want to designate the NKJV as the Bible Target Window. Click the Bible Target Window button in the NKJV window. Whenever you click a Ref Mark hot spot in another book (e.g., *Nelson's New Illustrated Bible Dictionary*), the NKJV will jump to the desired reference, regardless of which Bible you were most recently using.

> **NOTE:** You may select only *one* Bible as the "Target" window. If you try to select a second Bible window, the second window will become the new target window, the first one becoming unselected.

Arranging Books on Your Desktop

There are five ways to position your book windows on the screen: Cascading, Tiling Vertically, Tiling Horizontally, Minimizing as Icons, and manually resizing with the mouse.

Cascading Books

You can "cascade" the open windows, causing them to overlap each other on the screen. Because a portion of each window is always visible, you can bring any window to the "top," making it the active window by clicking with the mouse on any exposed portion of the desired window. The advantage of cascading as opposed to tiling is that all of your documents have equally large windows enabling you to work comfortably with them. The disadvantage is that you can see only one document at a time. To cascade the windows:

■ Click the Cascade button on the main Toolbar and the windows will "cascade" on the desktop.

■ Select *Cascade* from the **Window Menu** (ALT+W,C).

Tiling Books

You can "tile" the open windows, dividing your screen, either vertically or horizontally, into equally-sized windows. The advantage to tiling as opposed to cascading is that all of your documents are completely visible simultaneously. The disadvantage is that if you have more than two or three books open on your screen, each book will probably have too small a window to be very useful. To tile the windows:

■ Click the **Tile Vertically** button ⬚ on the Toolbar and the windows will tile vertically (ALT+W,V). Click the **Tile Horizontally** button

⬚ on the Toolbar and the windows will tile horizontally on the desktop (ALT+W,T).

■ Select *Tile Vertically* from the **Window Menu** and the windows will tile vertically on the desktop (ALT+W,V). Select *Tile Horizontally* from the **Window Menu** and the windows will tile horizontally on the desktop (ALT+W,T).

Arranging Icons

To minimize clutter on your screen you may want to minimize all but one or two of your open windows by clicking the Minimize button in the upper right corner of each window, making them icons. You can arrange the icons at the bottom of your screen. By reducing your open books to icons you can keep your screen clear for the one or two books that you are using at any given moment.

Whenever you want to consult one of the iconized books, merely double-click its icon at the bottom of the screen and it will open on the screen, returning to the same size and position it occupied when you last minimized it. When you want to look at a different book, minimize the current one if you wish and maximize the desired book. Working in this manner is akin to having dozens of books sitting on your desk, all with bookmarks holding your working position, ready at the click of a button to open for you.

To arrange your book icons:

■ Select *Arrange Icons* from the **Window Menu** (ALT+W,A).

Manually Resizing Document Windows

You can rearrange your document windows by manually resizing them with the mouse. Position the mouse cursor over any one of the four window borders and it will change into a double-ended arrow. Click and drag the desired border until the window is sized as desired. Click on the window's title bar to drag the window to a new location on the screen.

Altering a Book's Display

Once you have a document open in a window, there are a number of things you can do to manipulate the window and its display:

- **Move Window:** You can move the window to another place on the screen by clicking and dragging its title bar.

- **Expand/Shrink Window:** You can expand and shrink the window by clicking and dragging one or more of its borders.

- **Expand/Shrink Text:** You can expand and shrink the size of the text:

   To expand the text size select *Larger Text* from the **View Menu** (ALT+V,L) [CTRL+SHIFT+>].

   To shrink the text size select *Smaller Text* from the **View Menu** (ALT+V,M) [CTRL+SHIFT+<].

- **Change Text Font:** You can change the default text fonts and font sizes in any book to other fonts available on your system. See **Fonts** in chapter seven, "System Management."

- **Bible Text Only:** When viewing Bibles, select *Bible Text Only* from the **View** menu to display only Bible text verse by verse, without formatting or other editorial marks and headings (ALT+V,X).

Hot Spots

Within the text of a NEBRL electronic book, there are six possible types of highlighted text (i.e., text in a color other than that of the main text). Five of these are "hot spots," or text types which, when clicked with the mouse, will cause an action to take place. (When positioning the mouse cursor over one of the five hot spot text types, it will change into a hand cursor.)

The sixth type of highlighted text is merely red-colored text, which causes no action when clicked and is most often used to display the words of Jesus in red.

Two of the five hot spot text types can be found by opening the *Nelson's New Illustrated Bible Dictionary* to the article "Moon." (Fig. 3-13). (See **Opening Non-Bible Books** elsewhere in this chapter.)

Go Tos

These hot spots are often preceded by an asterisk (*). Clicking on a Go To hot spot will cause the book to "go to" that location. In the article "Moon" the word "calendar" is a Go To hot spot. Click "calendar" and the dictionary goes to the article "Calendar." (Click the **Backtrack** button on the main Toolbar to return to "Moon." See **Backtrack** elsewhere in this chapter.) Go To hot spots are normally red, but you can change their color in the General tab panel of the Preferences dialog.

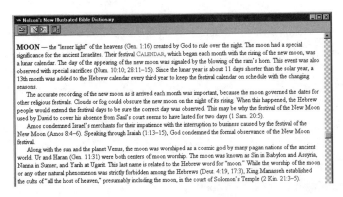

Figure 3-13 *Nelson's New Illustrated Bible Dictionary* Article on Moon.

Popups

These hot spots often indicate abbreviations, translator's notes, and cross references—all types of hidden text within the main text. This hidden text is accessed by clicking the popup hot spot, causing a popup window to appear. Clicking a second time anywhere on the screen will cause the popup window to disappear if it is a temporary popup window. If it is an information popup window, it will remain visible unless you click the close button in the upper left corner of the popup window. (You can cause all popups to be either temporary or information popups, by changing the default setting in the General tab panel of the Preferences dialog. See **Popup Windows** in chapter seven, "System Management.") Popup hot spots are normally green, but you can change their color in the General tab panel of the Preferences dialog.

Ref Marks

These Bible reference hot spots will cause a Bible to go to the indicated reference. In the article "Moon" one of the Ref Mark hot spots is "Gn. 1:16." Click the reference and a Bible will go to Genesis 1:16. Ref Mark hot spots are normally blue but their color can be changed in the General tab panel of the Preferences dialog. See Color in chapter seven, "System Management."

Which Bible goes to the verse? There are four possibilities:

- You have three different Bibles open on your screen. You have selected one of the Bibles to be the Bible Target Window. This is the Bible which will jump to the verse. (See **Bible Target Window** elsewhere in this chapter.)

- You have three different Bibles open on your screen. You have *not* selected any of the Bibles to be the Bible Target Window. However, you were most recently working in the KJV. It was the last Bible window to be active. This is the Bible which will jump to the verse.

- You have three different Bibles open on your screen. You have *not* selected any of the Bibles to be the Bible Target Window. However, you have linked the three Bibles together. All three Bibles will jump to the verse. (See **Linking Books** elsewhere in this chapter.)

- You have no Bibles open on your screen. Your "Preferred Bible" will be the one which opens and jumps to the verse. (See **Preferred Bible** in chapter seven, "System Management.")

Standardized Reference Hotspots

A Standardized Reference Hotspot is a hotspot that jumps to a particular location via a **Standardized Reference**. Some hotspots specify a book, whereas others do not.

If the hotspot doesn't specify a particular book to jump to, *Nelson's Electronic Bible Reference Library* will do whatever this SR's scheme is configured to do. To configure your SR schemes, use the **Standardized References Panel** in the **Preferences** dialog.

If the hotspot specifies a particular book to jump to, NEBRL will jump to the location specified by the SR within the specified book no matter how the scheme is configured. If the book doesn't exist, then the hotspot is treated as one which doesn't specify a book.

Notes and Macros

The two remaining types of hot spots are Notes and Macros. Click a Note hot spot to open a user-created note. Click a Macro hot spot to execute a user-created macro. Notes are discussed in chapter five, **Notes and Cross References**. Macros are discussed in **Toolbar** in chapter seven, "System Management."

Linking Books

The ability to link two or more books to each other is a powerful feature which enables you to move through multiple books in unison. Any book can be linked to any other book. Versified books (Bibles and Bible commentaries) are the most common types of books to link together. Linking a Notes or Search Results window to your current book is also very common. Books may also be linked based on any **Standardized References (SRs)** in them.

Versified books are linked based on the standard Bible reference number scheme which enables linking documents together based on their identical textual arrangement. In versified books NEBRL accounts for verse anomalies. For example, if you link the KJV to the Septuagint, they will scroll together based on the *content* of the verses, not the verse numbers which can differ between the two versions.

Notes are linked based on the text that each note refers to. This allows you to view the complete text of your notes along with the text that you have taken notes about.

Search Results windows are linked based on the articles you have search hits in. This allows you to view each of your search hits completely in their original context for a more complete understanding of what you are searching for. If the search results belong to a Bible, they will be linked according to the verses the search hits are in.

Books with **Standardized References (SRs)** can be linked and scrolled in parallel. You may link books that support the same SR scheme in the same fashion that you link any other windows.

Books are linked from the **Link** menu (Fig. 3-14).

Access the Link menu by doing either of the following:

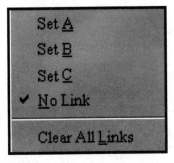

Figure 3-14 Link Menu.

■ Click the **Link** button on the Toolbar in each book window you want to include in the link set.

■ Select *Links* from the **Window** menu (ALT+W,L).

The **Link** menu will appear allowing you to assign the current book to one of three link sets: A, B, or C. You can create up to three different sets of linked windows. The one restriction is that a book can be a member of only one group at a time. Click Set A, Set B, or Set C to select the link set for the current book.

With Bible or commentary windows linked, moving to a verse in any one of the linked windows will cause the other member windows of the group to all move in unison to the same verse.

Link any book to your Note window. As you move through the book, the Note window will display the appropriate note attached to your current book location if one exists. Or, as you scroll through your notes, the book will jump to the locations where the notes are attached.

Link your Search Results window to other books so that as you scroll through the search results, the other books jump to the appropriate locations.

To remove a window from its link group:

- Make certain the window to be unlinked is active by clicking anywhere inside it. Click the **Link** button [image] on the document window Toolbar. Click *No Link*.

- Make certain the window to be unlinked is active by clicking anywhere inside it. Select *Links* from the **Window** menu (ALT+W,L). Click *No Link*.

To unlink all books:

- From the Link menu select *Clear All Links*. The windows will all scroll independently of each other.

Standardized References (SRs)

There are several types of books which are meant to be used in conjunction with other books organized in the same fashion. They share a common organizational scheme and thus can be scrolled in parallel. Just as Bibles are organized by book, chapter, and verse, these books have their own schemes of dividing and organizing their sections. Some books divide their text into articles, sections, and subsections. Plays divide their text into act, scene, and line.

One specific example of books with a common Standardized Reference (or SR) scheme is the Concordia Triglotta (books available from Logos): Three books, each a different translation of the same text. These three books are meant to be used in parallel. Such collections of books are organized in exactly the same fashion and thus share the same Standardized Reference scheme.

One other example of the use of SRs would be to view different editions of a famous play in parallel. Viewing them in parallel allows the user to instantaneously see the differences between the two (or more) editions.

Linking books with common SRs is easy. Simply open the books and link them using the Link button found on the toolbars of the book windows or by using the Link submenu found on the Window menu. Now when you move to other locations in one of the linked books, the other linked books will go to their parallel locations.

Bookmarks

As with printed books, NEBRL bookmarks allow you to mark your current location in a book so that you can return to it later. NEBRL allows you to set up to nine bookmarks.

Example: You are located at Exodus 12:37 in the active document window and you wish to move to other verses knowing that eventually you will return to Exodus 12:37. NEBRL allows you to set a bookmark at Exodus 12:37, making it easy to return to this verse at any time.

Setting a Bookmark

Assume you are located at Exodus 12:37 and you wish to set Bookmark 2 at this location. Set Bookmark 2 using either of these methods:

- Hold down the SHIFT key while clicking the **Bookmark 2** button on the Toolbar. (The default main Toolbar has five bookmark buttons. You can have up to nine bookmark buttons if you desire. To add the additional four Bookmark buttons to your Toolbar, you must customize the Toolbar so that it includes these buttons. See **Toolbar** in chapter seven, "System Management.")

- Select *Set* from the **Bookmark** menu. Click *2* to set Bookmark 2 (ALT+B,S,2).

Wherever you go in any of your books, you can return to Exodus 12:37 by accessing Bookmark 2. Bookmark 2 will stay set to Exodus 12:37 until you reset it to a different location.

Using Bookmarks

There are a number of ways you can access a Bookmark to return to a previous location in a book.

- Click the **Bookmark 2** button on the Toolbar. (The default main Toolbar has five bookmark buttons. You can have up to nine bookmark buttons if you desire. To add the additional four Bookmark buttons to your Toolbar, you must customize the Toolbar so that it includes these buttons. See **Toolbar** in chapter seven, "System Management.")

- Select *2* from the **Bookmark** menu (ALT+B,2).

- Select *Bookmark 0* from the **Bookmark** menu to return to your most recent previous location (ALT+B,0).

Backtrack

Backtrack moves you backwards through the list of articles already viewed during the current NEBRL session (since you last started NEBRL). Clicking this button repeatedly will eventually lead all the way back to the first article viewed after starting NEBRL.

Access this bookmark as follows:

- Click the **Backtrack** button on the Toolbar.

History

The History dialog displays all of the book locations to which you have jumped in the current NEBRL session (Fig. 3-15). Scroll down the list, click

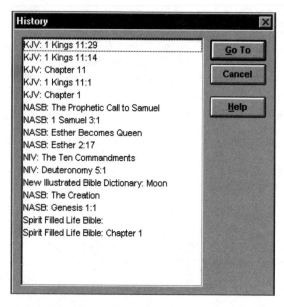

Figure 3-15 History Dialog.

the desired location, then click *Go To*.

Access the History dialog in one of the following ways:

- Click the **History** button on the Toolbar.
- Select *History* from the **Bookmark** menu (ALT+B,H) [CTRL+H].

Weights and Measure Calculator

NEBRL provides the **Weights and Measure Calculator** to assist you in converting various types of ancient units of weight and measure either to other ancient forms or modern forms (Fig. 3-16).

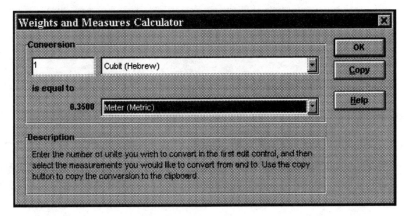

Figure 3-16 Weights and Measures Calculator Dialog.

To access the Weights and Measures Calculator:

1. Select *Weights and Measures Calculator* from the **Tools** menu (ALT+T,W).

2. Enter the number of units you want to convert in the first Conversion edit box. For example, to convert one cubit into meters, enter 1 in this box.

3. Using the down arrow next to the Conversion drop-down list box, scroll down the list to select "Cubit (Hebrew)."

4. Using the down arrow next to the Is Equal To drop-down list box, scroll down the list to select "Meter (Metric)." The answer, 0.3500, will display to the left.

5. Click *Copy* to copy the conversion to the Windows clipboard.

Catalog Cards (MARC Records)

Complete library information is available for all NEBRL electronic books through the **Catalog Cards (MARC Records)** dialog (Fig. 3-17).

To access the Catalog Cards (MARC Records) dialog:

1. Select *View Catalog Cards (MARC Records)* from the **Tools** menu (ALT+T,V).

2. Using the down arrow next to the Title to Show Cards For drop-down list box, scroll down the list to select a book.

3. Click one of the option buttons to select the display you want.

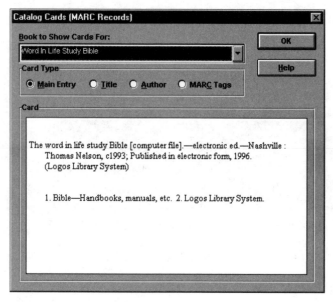

Figure 3-17 Catalog Cards (MARC Records) Dialog.

Returning Books to the Shelf

To delete, or close, a window:

1. Click the mouse anywhere in the target window, making it the active window.

2. Use either of the following methods to close the window:

   ■ Windows 3.1: Double-click the Control Menu Box in the upper left corner of the window. The active window will be closed and another one will be highlighted, becoming the active window.

   ■ Windows 95: Click the close box (the "X" box) in the upper *right* corner of the window.

   ■ Select *Close* from the **File** menu (ALT+F,C).

3. Select Tiling or Cascading from the **Window Menu** and the remaining windows will rearrange themselves accordingly.

Quitting NEBRL and Saving Your Files

Creating, opening, and saving note files is discussed in chapter five, "Notes and Cross References." However, for the sake of completeness, as we discuss how to quit NEBRL, we will assume you have created notes. As you quit NEBRL, if you have created notes, you will be asked if you want to save note file(s) for future use.

To Quit NEBRL:

1. Select *Exit Logos* from the **File** menu (ALT+F,X) [CTRL+Q or ALT+F4].

2. A dialog will appear asking if you want to save Notes before quitting. Click *Yes*.

3. If you have already given your note file a name, NEBRL will save your changes to the note file and then disappear from your screen. If your note file is new and unnamed, the **Save As** dialog will appear. Name your Note file with eight or fewer characters. NEBRL will automatically add the proper extension (.NOT). Click *OK* or, from the keyboard, press ENTER.

4. NEBRL will disappear from your screen.

4

Searching

Entering Search Mode

Basic Search Dialog

The NEBRL Search engine is a powerful tool which enables you to perform simple or complex searches on your entire library or specified portions of it quickly and efficiently.

You can enter Search mode in a number of ways:

- Press the **Search** button on the Toolbar.

- Select *Search* from the **Edit** menu (ALT+E,S) [ALT+S].

The basic Search dialog will appear (Fig. 4-1).

> NOTE: If you do not have versified books in your collection (Bibles, commentaries, etc.), a more abbreviated form of the Search dialog will appear.

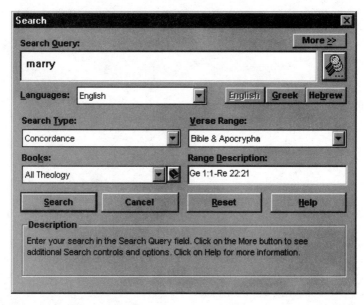

Figure 4-1 Basic Search Dialog.

Expanded Search Dialog

The basic Search dialog provides the features most commonly used for searching. Some advanced search features require the expanded Search dialog which is accessed by clicking the *More* button in the upper right corner of the basic Search dialog (Fig. 4-1). To return to the basic Search dialog, click the *Less* button in the upper right corner of the expanded Search dialog.

The expanded Search dialog provides access to Filter Searches, TVM and Morphology searches, a multitude of search options, and a search operators Help section (Fig. 4-2).

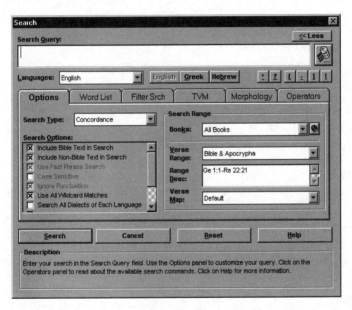

Figure 4-2 Expanded Search Dialog.

Search Basics

While the NEBRL search engine is extremely powerful, able to perform very complex searches in a multilingual environment, do not be intimidated by the smorgasbord of features available to you in the Search dialog. A novice NEBRL user can quickly perform a very simple search for a single word to find all of its occurrences in the library.

To perform a basic concordance search:

1. In the Search Query box, type the word for which you are searching. (In Fig. 4-1 the word "marry" is entered in the Search Query box.)

2. Click *Search*. NEBRL will search through your entire library to locate all occurrences of that word.

When you wish to perform a more complicated search, NEBRL accommodates you with easy-to-use search *operators*. There are two kinds of search operators: *Type operators* and *Boolean operators*. They are both discussed later in this chapter.

Have Fun . . . Then *Reset!*

Begin experimenting with the varied features of the NEBRL search engine. Click any check boxes, choose any option, type in any box . . . have fun— and learn. At any time, you can reset the entire search engine back to the NEBRL preset defaults by clicking *Reset* (Fig. 4-1).

> **NOTE:** After you have performed a search, the next time you re-open the Search dialog (assuming you have not quit and restarted NEBRL), your most recent search parameters will still be selected. That is, if you were to open the Search dialog and click *Search*, the most recent search would be performed again. If your next search is vastly different from your previous one, it may be safer to click *Reset* before you select new options, so as to start fresh from the default Search dialog. This can prevent undesirable search results due to lingering search options from previous searches that you may have forgotten were still selected.

Figure 4-3 Word Browser.

Word Browser Search

The Word Browser search is another fast and easy way to perform a concordance search. It bypasses the Search dialog and searches directly from the Word Browser which contains a list of every unique word in your NEBRL electronic library (Fig. 4-3).

To access the Word Browser:

■ Select *Word Browser* from the **View** menu (ALT+V,W) [CTRL+W].

To search from the Word Browser:

1. Select a language from the Language drop-down list box. Access the list box by

clicking the **Language** button .

2. Select a search word by entering it in the Search For box or by scrolling down the list to locate the word you want. (Scroll quickly down the list by dragging the vertical scroll button with the mouse.) A list of matching articles will appear in the Articles list box. Select the desired article and click the *View Selection* button or double-click on the article title.

> **NOTE:** You can also initiate a right-mouse-menu concordance search from the Word Browser. Since the Word Browser browses either the book of your choice or all books in your library, probably the two reasons for executing a right-mouse-menu concordance search from the Browser are: (1) The right-mouse-menu gives you the added option of searching *all open books* rather than *all* books in your library. Therefore, you can easily limit your search to the books which are open on your screen rather than one or all. (2) You can see your hits in context in the Search Results window. This may assist you in more quickly locating appropriate hits.

To close the Word Browser, click the Close button in the upper corner of the window (Windows 3.1, left corner; Windows 95, right corner).

Search Range

When you perform a search, NEBRL will search your currently active book unless you specify otherwise.

For each search, you can specify a search range, that is, the group of books you want to search. The search range includes both which books should be searched, as well as the range of Bible passages in Bibles.

Example: If you know that the information you seek is in the Old Testament, you can restrict your search of Bibles to the Old Testament. You may specify a range of verses, chapters, or books, up to the entire Bible, as the text to be searched.

Defining User Preset Search Ranges

Rather than defining the list of books and Bible passages to be searched every time you perform a search, you can create Preset Search Ranges, ranges of books and/or Bible passages you most commonly want to search. Then, when you define a search, set the search range to one of your preset ranges.

Make changes to the default list of Preset Search Ranges supplied with NEBRL in the **Define Preset Ranges** dialog (Fig. 4-4). To open this dialog, do the following:

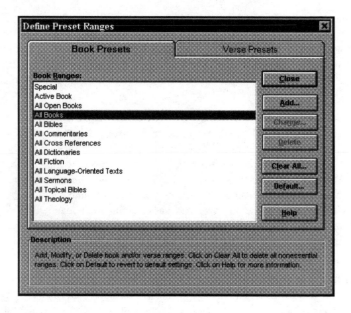

Figure 4-4 Define Preset Ranges Dialog.

■ Open the **Define Preset Ranges** dialog by selecting *Preset Search Ranges* from the **Edit** menu (ALT+E,E).

The Define Preset Ranges dialog has two tab folders: Book Presets, used for defining groups of books as search ranges; and Verse Presets, used for defining groups of Bible passages as search ranges within Bibles.

Book Presets

NEBRL supplies a collection of Book Preset Search Ranges: Active Book, All Open Books, All Books, All Bibles, All Commentaries, All Dictionaries, etc. You may create your own Book Presets, modify existing presets, or delete them.

> **NOTE:** You cannot delete the following four preset book ranges: Special, Active Book, All Open Books, and All Books.

To create a new Book Preset called "Favorite Bibles," which will contain the King James Version and the Contemporary English Version, do the following:

1. After opening the Define Preset Ranges dialog, you will be in the Book Presets tab folder. To add a new book preset, click *Add*. The **Define Book Range** dialog will open (Fig. 4-5).

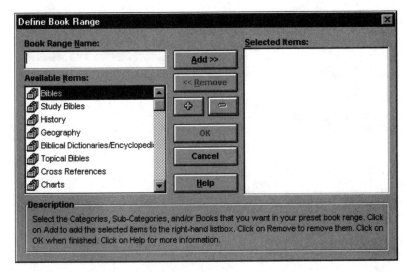

Figure 4-5 Define Book Range Dialog.

2. In the Book Range Name box, type:

   Favorite Bibles

3. In the Available Items list, click on the category Bibles to highlight it. Click the plus sign (+) to expand the category and see the list of Bibles available, or merely double-click on Bibles. Click the minus sign (–) to collapse the list again, or double-click Bibles.

4. With the category Bibles expanded, select the NKJV by clicking on it and clicking *Add* to add it to the Selected Items list on the right. Do the same for the KJV (Fig. 4-6).

5. If you add items to the Selected Items list that you later decide to remove from the list, click on the item to be deleted, and then click *Remove*.

6. When the list contains the items you desire for your new Book Preset Search Range, click *OK*. You will be returned to the main dialog and your new Book Preset will have been added to the list.

7. You may modify an existing Book Preset. Click on it to highlight it, then click *Change* to reopen the Define Book Range dialog.

8. You may delete an existing Book Preset. Click on it to highlight it, then click *Delete* to delete it.

9. Click *Clear All* to delete all nonessential ranges. Click *Default* to revert to default settings.

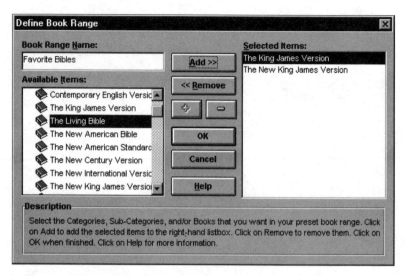

Figure 4-6 KJV and NKJV Defined as Favorite Bibles Preset Range.

Verse Presets

To create, modify, or delete Verse Preset Search Ranges, click the Verse Presets tab in the Define Preset Ranges dialog. NEBRL supplies a list of default Verse Preset Search Ranges (Fig. 4-7).

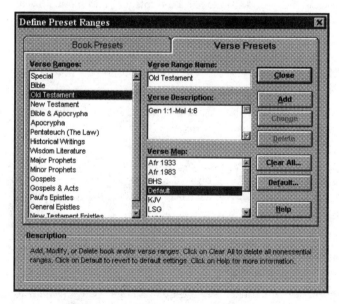

Figure 4-7 Verse Preset Search Ranges.

To create a new Verse Preset called "Prophets," which will contain all of the Old Testament prophetical writings, both "major" and "minor," do the following:

1. Click the Verse Presets tab folder. To add a new verse preset, in the Verse Range Name box, type:

    Prophets

2. In the Verse Description box, type:

    Is-Mal

3. Click *Add* to add your new Verse Range to the Verse Ranges list on the left (Fig. 4-8).

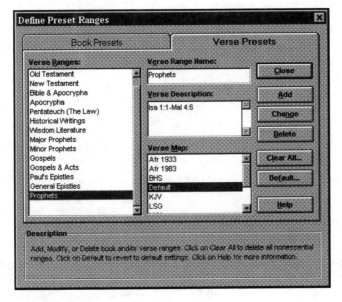

Figure 4-8 Adding Prophets Verse Range.

4. You may modify an existing Verse Range Preset. Click on it to highlight it. Make the desired changes in the Verse Description box, then click *Change* to make your changes permanent.

5. You may delete an existing Verse Range Preset. Click on it to highlight it, then click *Delete* to delete it.

6. Click *Clear All* to delete all nonessential ranges. Click *Default* to revert to default settings.

Search Ranges and Bibles with Alternate Book Orders

Using predefined Verse Ranges or typing a custom Verse Range that uses hyphens to indicate a range of books in the Verse Range field of the Search Dialog will not always produce expected results. NEBRL uses the book order of the King James Version of the Bible for predefined search ranges. Several Bibles use book orders different than the King James Version, including, but not limited to the Tanakh, the Septuagint, and the Biblia Hebraica Stuttgartensia.

If you are having difficulty expressing a range of books and finding correct results, try listing each book title individually in the Verse Range field.

Selecting a Search Range

With the Search dialog open, select your search range from either the Books list box or the Verse Range list box.

Point and Click Range Selection

To select a Search Range:

1. If you have a Book Preset Search Range (see **Defining Preset Search Ranges**), click the down arrow next to the Books list box. Click the desired Book Preset to select it.

2. If you need to create a special book range for a particular search, click

   the Book button next to the Books list box. The **Search Range** dialog will open (Fig. 4-9).

3. In the Available Items browser, select the categories, subcategories, and/or books that you want to search. As you click on each one, highlighting it, click *Add* to add the selected category/book to the Selected Items list box on the right. Highlight and click *Remove* to remove any from the Selected Items list. Click *OK* to return to the main Search dialog when your special book range is complete.

4. After defining the books to be searched, if Bibles are included among the books, you can also define a verse range to be used when searching Bibles. If there is an appropriate Verse Preset Search Range available, click the arrow next to the Verse Range list box. Click the appropriate Verse Preset to select it. The Range Description box will display the verses that match the verse range you have selected.

5. If you need to create a special verse range (e.g., Exodus from Egypt, Ex 12:37–51), type "Ex 12:37–51" (without quotes) in the Range Description

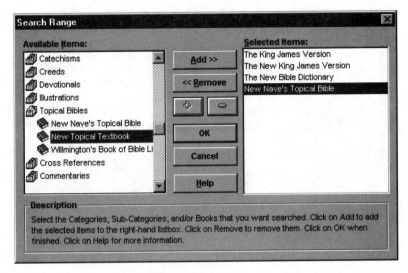

Figure 4-9 Search Range Dialog.

box (Fig. 4-1). If you type in a special range, the Verse Range box will display the word "Special."

6. Leave the Verse Map as Default unless you specifically want to utilize the verse mapping from the non-standard versified books.

Drag and Drop Range Selection

"Drag and drop" means to click a highlighted item with the left mouse button and, while holding down the button, drag the item to another location on the screen where it is "dropped" by releasing the mouse button.

To select a Search Range using drag and drop techniques, do one of the following:

■ Click a book title in the main Library Browser, highlighting it. Drag the book title to the Books box in the Search Range section of the Options panel and drop it there (Fig. 4-10). The word "Special" will appear in the box. If you click the Book button ▨ next to the Books box, the Search Range dialog will open (Fig. 4-9) and you will see the dragged book in the Selected Items list box. To select more than one book for your special search range, *hold down the* SHIFT *key* while you drag and drop each book into the Books box.

■ In the Search dialog, click the Book button ▨ next to the Books box. The Search Range dialog will open (Fig. 4-9). From the Available Items

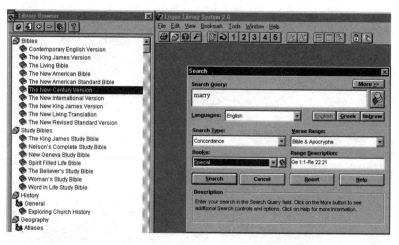

Figure 4-10 Drag and Drop Book Into Search Range Books Box.

list box, select categories, subcategories, and books by clicking them. Drag and drop each selected category, subcategory, or book over to the Selected Items list box where it will be added to the search range list. When using this dialog, all of the books you drag to the Selected Items box will automatically be *added* to the list without the need for holding down the SHIFT key.

Right Mouse Range Selection

To select a Search Range using the right mouse menu, do the following:

■ In the Search dialog, click the Book button ▨ next to the Books box. The Search Range dialog will open (Fig. 4-9). From the Available Items list box, select categories, subcategories, and books by *right*-clicking them. The right mouse menu will open. Click on *Expand Item* to expand a category (⌖+E). Click *Add Item* to add the item to the Selected Items box (⌖+A). To remove an item from your search range, right-click on the item in the Selected Items box. From the right mouse menu click *Remove Item* (⌖+R).

Type Operators

Once you have selected the *range* for your search, you must select a search *type*. NEBRL supports five basic types of searches: Concordance, Phrase, Topic, Reference, and Filter searches. NEBRL defaults to concordance searching. The other four types of searches utilize *type operators*. Type operators are search operators which define the type of search to be performed. If a type operator is not used, NEBRL assumes a concordance search.

> **NOTE:** While NEBRL normally assumes a concordance search, be aware that after you have performed a search, the next time you reopen the Search dialog (assuming you have not quit and restarted NEBRL), your most recent search parameters will still be selected. That is, if you were to open the Search dialog and click *Search*, the most recent search would be performed again. If your next search is vastly different from your previous one, it may be safer to click *Reset* before you select new options, so as to start fresh from the default Search dialog. This can prevent undesirable search results due to lingering search options from previous searches that you may have forgotten were still selected.

Concordance (Word) Search

This is the default and most commonly-used search type. A concordance search is a search by whole word unit. The concordance search allows you to search for occurrences of any word in a single book, a group of books, or your entire library. When you perform a search, NEBRL will search your currently active book unless you specify otherwise.

To search for every occurrence of the word "marry" in your active book, merely type in the Search Query box:

    marry

Ensure that the Search Type is set to Concordance, then click *Search*. If you have left the search range set to its default, Active Book, NEBRL will find every instance of the word "marry" in your currently active book.

If you do not want to limit your search to your active book, change the search range appropriately. Default preset search ranges available include: Active Book (the book you were working in before you accessed the Search dialog), All Open Books (the books currently open on your screen), All Books, All Dictionaries, All Encyclopedias, etc. (See **Search Range**.)

Phrase Search

The Phrase Search is a search for a phrase or partial phrase within a book. This search looks for an exact match to what you type.

To search for the phrase "and God said" in the Pentateuch of the King James Version:

1. Click in the Search Query box and type:

        and God said

2. Change the Book Range to the KJV.

3. Change the Verse Range to Pentateuch (The Law).

4. To select Phrase as the search type, do either of the following:

- Click the down arrow next to the Search Type list box. From the list select Phrase by clicking it.

- To use the phrase type operator, click in the Search Query box and type:

  ```
  PHRASE(and God said) or phrase(and God said)
  ```

  Instead of typing "phrase(...)" you can abbreviate the phrase type operator by typing "ph(...)."

5. Click *Search*. NEBRL will search only the Pentateuch in the KJV for all occurrences of "and God said."

Fast Phrase Search

The Phrase Search typically takes quite a bit longer to execute than a simple concordance search for a single word. However, NEBRL offers a high-speed version of Phrase Search called Fast Phrase Search. Fast Phrase Search is extremely quick, but because of its speed, it may occasionally include a hit which contains an extra word not included in the phrase for which you are searching.

To access Fast Phrase Search:

- Select Phrase from the Search Type box in the Search dialog, and then click the Use Fast Phrase Search box in the Search Options list. (This option is already selected by default.)

Topic Search

The Topic search is a search for a topic within a book(s). These topics are generally associated with book articles, chapters, or major headings within chapters. (The topic search was formerly known as the "key" or "key phrase" search. The word "key" is still supported and may be used instead of "topic" if you so desire.)

Example: A chapter in a book may discuss the roles of husbands and wives within the home. While the word "marriage" may not actually exist in the chapter text, the topics "marriage," "husband," "wife," and "home" may have been assigned to the chapter.

To search for the topic "marriage" in the entire library:

1. Click in the Search Query box and type:

   ```
   marriage
   ```

2. Change the Book Range to All Books.

3. Change the Verse Range to Bible so that all articles within all Bibles will be searched.

4. To select Topic as the search type, do either of the following:

- Click the down arrow next to the Search Type list box. From the list select Topic by clicking it and then type:

   ```
   marriage
   ```

- To use the topic type operator, click in the Search Query box and type:

   ```
   TOPIC(marriage) or topic(marriage) or
   top(marriage)
   ```

5. Click *Search*. NEBRL will search all topically-indexed books for chapters, articles, or chapter sections keyed to the topic "marriage."

Reference Search

The Reference search finds all occurrences of the Bible reference specified (e.g., Exodus 12:37) within a book(s). This is a search for the actual reference, "Exodus 12:37," *not* the text of the verse. NEBRL will locate all occurrences of the reference Exodus 12:37, even if they are spelled "Ex 12:37," "Ex. 12.37," "12.37," "v. 37," etc.

To search for every occurrence of the reference Exodus 12:37 within the *Nelson's New Illustrated Bible Dictionary*:

1. Click in the Search Query box and type:

   ```
   Ex 12:37
   ```

2. Change the Book Range to *Nelson's New Illustrated Bible Dictionary*.

3. To select Reference as the search type, do the following:

- To use the reference type operator, click in the Search Query box and type:

   ```
   REF(Ex 12:37) or ref(Ex 12:37)
   ```

4. Click *Search*. NEBRL will search the *Nelson's New Illustrated Bible Dictionary* for all occurrences of the reference Exodus 12:37.

Filter Search

The Filter search tab panel, located in the expanded Search dialog (see **Expanded Search Dialog**), enables you to extract all of the Bible verses which are mentioned in a particular article of a particular book. That is, the list of all verses in the Bible has been "filtered" by the book or article to a smaller list of verses more relevant for your purpose. This smaller list of relevant verses is the list that is then searched in the Bible(s) or your choice for whatever word or phrase you desire.

Example

Locate all of the verses which relate to Aaron's rod and also mention Moses in the KJV. It is not satisfactory to merely search for verses which have the words "rod" and "Moses" in them, which could yield verses about a rod other than Aaron's, or might miss verses which are involved in the discussion of Aaron's rod, but which do not actually have the word "rod" in the verse.

Use a Filter search to help solve the problem:

1. In the Filter search panel, select the category Dictionaries. Select the *Nelson's New Illustrated Bible Dictionary*. The Choose By Topic button becomes highlighted because the *Nelson's New Illustrated Bible Dictionary* has topics assigned to its articles.

2. Click **Choose By Topic**. The Choose Filter Topic Browser opens.

3. Click the topic, "Aaron's Rod." The matching article, "Aaron's Rod," becomes highlighted.

4. Click **Select**, returning you to the main Filter search panel.

5. Click **Add**. The search type operator and its operand, FILTER(NBD,512), is added to the Search Query box. This operand tells NEBRL to use the *Nelson's New Illustrated Bible Dictionary* article 512 (Aaron's Rod) to provide the list of Bible verses for the next part of the search.

6. Finish typing the search query as follows:

   ```
   FILTER(NBD,512) AND Moses
   ```

7. Set your Search Range to the KJV. (After filtering the list of verses using the *Nelson's New Illustrated Bible Dictionary* on Aaron's Rod, you must then search the text of the verses in a particular Bible(s) for mention of Moses.)

8. Click **Search**. NEBRL will search through all of the KJV verses mentioned in the article "Aaron's Rod" to find those which also have the word "Moses" in them.

Example

Using the *New Nave's Topical Bible* in a Filter search is an extremely powerful tool. If you use the standard Concordance search for the word "Paul" in the KJV, NEBRL will find 163 occurrences. However, if you include a Filter search of the *New Nave's* topic "Paul" in the search as well, NEBRL will find 364 verses! This is due to the fact that there are many verses which refer to Paul using a word other than "Paul" (e.g., "Saul," "he," and "the apostle"). Because *New Nave's* includes these verses under the topic "Paul," they will be found!

To search the KJV New Testament for all verses containing the word "Paul," and include the verses listed by *Nave's* in the topic "Paul," do the following:

1. In the Filter search panel, select the category Topical Bibles. Select the *New Nave's Topical Bible*. The Choose By Topic button becomes highlighted because the *New Nave's* has topics assigned to its articles.

2. Click **Choose By Topic**. The Choose Filter Topic Browser opens.

3. Click the topic, "Paul." Click the matching article, "Paul," highlighting it.

4. Click **Select**, returning you to the main Filter search panel.

5. Click **Add**. The search type operator and its operand, FILTER(NEW-NAVES,4745), is added to the Search Query box. This operand tells NEBRL to use the *New Nave's* article 4745 (Paul) to provide the list of Bible verses for the next part of the search.

6. Finish typing the search query as follows:

   `FILTER(NEWNAVES,4745) OR Paul`

7. Set your Search Range to the KJV. (After filtering the list of verses using the *New Nave's* article on Paul, you must then search the text of the KJV for mention of Paul to see if there are additional verses to add to the list from the *Nave's* article.)

8. Click **Search**. NEBRL will find and return all verses in the KJV New Testament which contain the word "Paul" and all the verses listed in the *Nave's* topic "Paul" and its subtopics. NEBRL finds and returns 364 verses in all.

Previous Searches

A list of your previous searches can be found in the **Previous Searches** dialog (Fig. 4-11).

Open this dialog by doing the following:

- Click the Previous Searches button located to the right of the Search Query box.

Selecting any of the previous searches listed here will select not only the search text, but all properties of the previous search, such as search range, search type, and search options.

Clicking the Use Expanded Search Query box inserts the actual previous search query as understood by the NEBRL search engine into the Search Query box.

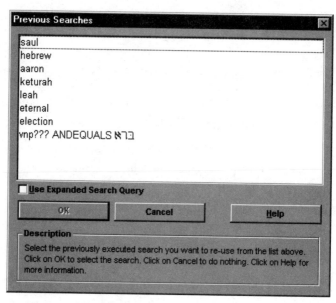

Figure 4-11 Previous Searches Dialog.

Example:

For your previous search you entered in the Search Query box the following:

    go?d

You also unchecked the Use All Wildcard Matches box (in Search Options) causing the **Choose Wildcard Matches** dialog to appear. You clicked "gold" and "good" as the words to be used in the search. You performed the search. NEBRL searched for "gold OR good."

After performing a few other searches you decide to reexecute the search on "gold OR good." You open the Previous Searches dialog. The previous search displays as "gold OR good" as the actual search command which was performed. However, if you click on "gold OR good" and then click **OK**, the search command will be entered into the Search Query box as "go?d" because this was the actual command you originally entered. This gives you the ability to select different possibilities from the Choose Wildcard Matches dialog again (assuming you have the Use All Wildcard Matches box unchecked). Perhaps this time you want to search on "gold OR goad OR good" instead. If you want to execute the exact same search again ("gold OR good"), click the Use Expanded Search Query box and the actual search as it was originally performed ("gold OR good") will be reentered into the Search Query box.

Search Options

The Search Options tab panel is located in the expanded Search dialog (see **Expanded Search Dialog**). Following is a list of the options available. Not all of these options are available for every type of search.

Include Bible Text in Search

Check this box if you want to include Bible text in your search. Unchecking this box allows you to search a Bible's book introductions, translators' notes, topical articles, etc. without also searching the Bible text itself.

Include Non-Bible Text in Search

Check this box if you want to include non-Bible text in your search. Unchecking this box allows you to search Bible text only, without also searching through the Bible's book introductions, section headings, translators' notes, topical articles, etc.

Fast Phrase Search

This search option is available only when executing phrase searches. Otherwise, it is greyed. Check this box to perform a Fast Phrase Search. It is checked by default. (See **Fast Phrase Search**.)

Case Sensitive

This search option is available only when executing phrase searches (but not Fast Phrase Searches). Otherwise, it is greyed. Check this box to perform a case-sensitive phrase search where the capitilization of words in the phrase is critical.

Example: In a search of the KJV for the phrase "and God said," if this search is case sensitive, NEBRL will find only one matching verse, Genesis 1:28, because the other 23 verses have "And," not "and."

Ignore Punctuation

This search option is available only when executing phrase searches (but not Fast Phrase Searches). Check this box to ignore all punctuation within the phrase for which you are searching. Uncheck this box to search for text with the punctuation exactly as you supply it in the Search Query box.

Use All Wildcard Matches

This search option is available when executing both Concordance and Topic searches. When using search wildcards (discussed later in this chapter), the search may find several wildcard matches, some of which you may not want to use. Checking this box tells NEBRL to automatically use all of the wildcard matches it finds without first showing them to you. If this box is unchecked, before NEBRL begins a search, it will first display all of the wildcard matches in the **Choose Wildcard Matches** dialog, thus allowing you to select the words for which you want to search by single-clicking on each one (Fig. 4-12).

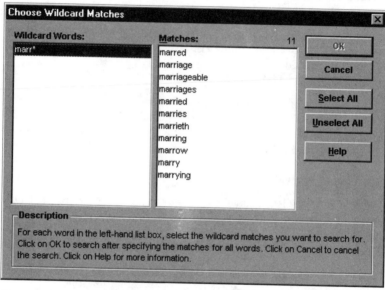

Figure 4-12 Choose Wildcard Matches Dialog.

Search All Dialects of Each Language

Checking this box enables all dialects of a language. For example, when you are searching books in English, you probably want NEBRL to include books written in UK English, Australian English, Canadian English, Eire English, and New Zealand English as well. NEBRL distinguishes between these dialects as distinct languages, but by checking this box NEBRL will include all of these dialects in an English search.

Search Across Languages

Checking this box tells NEBRL to search throughout all languages present in the books you are searching. For example, if you are searching for the word "die," NEBRL would find a match on the English word "die" and the German article "die." With this box unchecked, and if the search were in English, only the English word "die" would be found.

Show Books' Hits in Context

Checking this box automatically causes the Search Results window to open with the splitter bar in place and the search hit reference list (on the left) and context lines (on the right) expanded, as if you had clicked the Search

Results toolbar button **Show Hits in Context** .

Auto-Expand Hit Lists

Checking this box automatically causes the Search Results window to open with the search hit reference list automatically expanded (but not the context lines).

Word List

The **Word List** tab panel is located in the expanded Search dialog (see **Expanded Search Dialog**). It displays the Global Word List, a list of all words in all of the books in your library (Fig. 4-13).

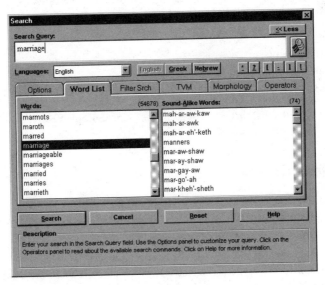

Figure 4-13 Search Dialog: Word List Tab Panel.

Every time you add new books to your NEBRL library, you should rebuild the Global Word List so that any new words contained in the new books will be added to the list. This list is for your benefit—it is *not* used by the search engine. It provides a visual list of all existing words so that you can visually scroll through the list to locate possible other forms of the words you seek.

To use the Word List:

1. Click the Word List tab to make the panel visible.

2. Begin typing a word in the Search Query box. NEBRL will scroll the Global Word List for words that start with the characters that you are typing. For example, if you type "marr," several words will be listed, among them being "marred," "marriage," and "marriages."

3. Select the word you want to use from either the Words list or the Sound-Alike Words list by clicking it with the mouse (Fig. 4-13). Clicking a word in the list to highlight it will automatically load it into the Search Query box.

TVM

The TVM tab panel is located in the expanded Search dialog (see **Expanded Search Dialog**). It enables you to search the KJV according to the Tense, Voice, and Mood of the Greek and Hebrew behind the KJV text. (See **TVM Search** in chapter eight, "Greek and Hebrew Study Tools.")

Morphology

The Morphology tab panel is located in the expanded Search dialog (see **Expanded Search Dialog**). It enables you to search Greek and Hebrew texts according to parts of speech. (See **Morphology Search** in chapter eight, "Greek and Hebrew Study Tools.")

Boolean Operators

In addition to the search *type* operators, NEBRL utilizes *boolean* operators which allow you to easily perform complex and highly specific searches on texts.

> **NOTE:** When using boolean operators, make certain that the *Concordance* search type is selected in the Search Type box. Also, make certain that you specify the desired search range just as you would with any other search.

Following is a list of the available search operators, a brief description of each, and an example. The search operators are listed in order of precedence; the first operator has the highest precedence, and the last has the lowest precedence. You may also group search clauses together by using parentheses.

AND

The AND Operator is a boolean operator. It will find all articles and/or verses which contain both the first and the second search terms. The AND operator can be used while searching both Bibles and non-Bibles.

Syntax

```
<search term> AND <search term>
```

Example

You may string together multiple terms with multiple ANDs:

```
Abraham AND Isaac AND Jacob
```

In Bibles this search will find all verses which have the words "Abraham," "Isaac," and "Jacob." In non-Bibles this search will find all articles which have these three words.

OR

The OR Operator is a boolean operator. It will find all articles and/or verses which contain either the first or the second search terms, or both of them. The OR operator can be used while searching both Bibles and non-Bibles.

Syntax

```
<search term> OR <search term>
```

Example

You may string together multiple terms with multiple ORs:

```
Abraham OR Isaac OR Jacob
```

In Bibles this search will find all verses which have any one, two, or all of the words "Abraham," "Isaac," and "Jacob." That is, a verse which has only "Abraham" is a match. A verse which has both "Abraham" and "Jacob" is also a match, and so on. In non-Bibles this search will find all articles which have any one, two, or all of these three words.

ANDNOT

The ANDNOT Operator is a boolean operator. It will find all articles and/or verses which contain the first search term, but not the second term.

The ANDNOT operator can be used while searching both Bibles and non-Bibles.

Syntax

```
<search term> ANDNOT <search term>
```

Example

```
Abraham ANDNOT Isaac
```

In Bibles this search will find all verses which have the word "Abraham," but not "Isaac." In non-Bibles this search will find all articles which have "Abraham," but not "Isaac."

XOR

The XOR Operator is a boolean operator. It will find all articles and/or verses which contain either the first search term or the second term, but not both. The XOR operator can be used while searching both Bible and non-Bible text.

Syntax

```
<search term> XOR <search term>
```

Example

```
Abraham XOR Isaac
```

In Bibles this search will find all verses which have either the word "Abraham" or "Isaac," but not both. While the XOR appears similar to OR, the difference lies in the fact that when using OR, a verse is a match if it contains either "Abraham" or "Isaac" or both "Abraham" and "Isaac." When using XOR the verse with both "Abraham" and "Isaac" would not be a match. In non-Bibles this search will find all articles which have either of these two words, but not both.

ANDEQUALS

The ANDEQUALS Operator is a boolean operator. It will find all occurrences of the first search term which are in the identical spot in the text as the second term. The ANDEQUALS operator can be used while searching both Bible and non-Bible text. Its function is unchanged whether working in Bible or non-Bible text.

Syntax

```
<search term> ANDEQUALS <search term>
```

Example

In the King James text, Strong's numbers are embedded within the text. For example, in Genesis 1:1 if you right-click the word "created," then click *Information*, you will find that the Strong's number 1254 is attached to the word "created." In the Search Languages box select Hebrew Strong's Numbers. In the Search Query box, enter:

```
1254
```

Change the language to English either by selecting English in the Language box or by merely clicking the *English* button (located next to the Language box). (This English button is for convenience because often you are switching back to English from other languages.) Click the cursor in the Search Query box after the 1254 you have already entered and type:

```
ANDEQUALS created
```

The entire search query displays as follows:

```
1254 ANDEQUALS created
```

NEBRL will find all occurrences of the Strong's number 1254 which are translated as "created." This is useful because 1254 is also translated as "make," "cut down," "choose," etc.

NOTEQUALS

The NOTEQUALS Operator is a boolean operator. It will find all occurrences of the first search term which are not in the identical spot in the text as the second term. The NOTEQUALS operator can be used while searching both Bible and non-Bible text. Its function is unchanged whether working in Bible or non-Bible text.

Syntax

```
<search term> NOTEQUALS <search term>
```

Example

In the King James text, Strong's numbers are embedded within the text. In Gensis 1:1, for example, if you right-click the word "created," then click *Information*, you will find that the Strong's number 1254 is attached to the word "created." In the Search Languages box select Hebrew Strong's Numbers. In the Search Query box, enter:

```
1254
```

Change the language to English either by selecting English in the Language box or by merely clicking the *English* button (located next to the Language box). (This English button is for convenience because often you are switching back to English from other languages.) Click the cursor in the Search Query box after the 1254 you have already entered and type:

        NOTEQUALS created

The entire search query displays as follows:

        1254 NOTEQUALS created

NEBRL will find all occurrences of the Strong's number 1254 which are not translated as "created." This is useful because 1254 is also translated as "make," "cut down," "choose," etc.

WITHINWORD

Finds all occurrences of the search terms within X words of each other. This search operator works the same way in Bibles and non-Bibles.

Syntax

        <search term> WITHINWORD 5 <search term>

Example

        Moses WITHINWORD 5 Aaron

In Bibles and non-Bibles this search will find all occurrences of the word "Moses" within 5 words of (before or after) "Aaron."

BEFOREWORD

Finds all occurrences of the search terms where the first search term occurs within X words before the second search term. This search operator works the same way in Bibles and non-Bibles.

Syntax

        <search term> BEFOREWORD 5 <search term>

Example

        Moses BEFOREWORD 5 Aaron

In Bibles and non-Bibles this search will find all occurrences of the word "Moses" within 5 words before "Aaron."

AFTERWORD

Finds all occurrences of the search terms where the first search term occurs within X words after the second search term.

Syntax

```
<search term> AFTERWORD 5 <search term>
```

Example

```
Moses AFTERWORD 5 Aaron
```

In Bibles and non-Bibles this search will find all occurrences of the word "Moses" within 5 words after "Aaron."

WITHINVERSE

Finds all occurrences of the search terms within X verses of each other. This search operator works only in Bibles.

Syntax

```
<search term> WITHINVERSE 5 <search term>
```

Example

```
Moses WITHINVERSE 5 Aaron
```

In Bibles this search will find all occurrences of the word "Moses" within 5 verses of (before or after) "Aaron."

BEFOREVERSE

Finds all occurrences of the search terms where the first search term occurs within X verses before the second search term. This search operator works only in Bibles.

Syntax

```
<search term> BEFOREVERSE 5 <search term>
```

Example

```
Moses BEFOREVERSE 5 Aaron
```

In Bibles this search will find all occurrences of the word "Moses" within 5 verses before "Aaron."

AFTERVERSE

Finds all occurrences of the search terms where the first search term occurs within X verses after the second search term. This search operator works only in Bibles.

Syntax

```
<search term> AFTERVERSE 5 <search term>
```

Example

```
Moses AFTERVERSE 5 Aaron
```

In Bibles this search will find all occurrences of the word "Moses" within 5 verses after "Aaron."

Combining Different Search Types

Although using boolean operators requires that the *Concordance* search type is selected in the Search Type box, NEBRL allows you to use the boolean operators with both Concordance and Phrase searches.

Example

Find all verses that say "And God said" or "And He said." Type:

```
PH(And God said) OR PH(And He said)
```

Example

Find all verses containing both the phrase "And God said" and the word "people." Type:

```
PH(And God said) and people
```

NOTE: Even though you are combining boolean operators with Concordance and Phrase searches, make certain that the *Concordance* search type is selected in the Search Type box (located on the Options panel). The Phrase search is not case-sensitive when doing combined searching. Also, make certain that you specify the desired search range just as you would with any other search.

Group Delimiters

The "parentheses" are group delimiters. You may group search clauses together by using parentheses.

Example

Find all verses that have either "Moses" or "Pharaoh" or both of them, but not "Aaron," which occur within nine verses of one containing "Israel." Type:

```
((Moses or Pharaoh) ANDNOT Aaron) WITHINVERSE 9
Israel
```

Wildcards and Character Classes

You can search for words in the Bible using wildcards and character classes expressions. Following is a discussion of the asterisk and question mark wildcards as well as the method for specifying character classes.

Asterisk Wildcard

Wildcards can be used only with Concordance searching. The asterisk wildcard (*) matches zero or more of any characters. Enter the asterisk from the keyboard, or click the **Asterisk** button located in the expanded Search dialog below the Search Query box (Fig. 4-2).

Example

```
rain*
```

Finds and returns all text containing words starting with "rain" and ending with any number of characters (e.g., "rain," "rainbow," "rained," etc.).

```
*ness
```

Finds and returns all text containing words ending with "ness" (e.g., "godliness," "goodness," etc.).

```
b*g
```

Finds and returns all text containing words beginning with "b" and ending with "g" (e.g., "bearing," "bag," "beginning," etc.).

Question Mark Wildcard

Wildcards can be used only with Concordance searching. The question mark wildcard (?) matches one and only one character. You can have one or more question mark wildcards. Also, you can have a search word with both question marks and asterisks. Enter the question mark from the keyboard, or click the **Question Mark** button located in the Search dialog below the Search Query box (Fig. 4-1).

```
j???
```

Finds and returns all text containing four-letter words starting with "j" (e.g., "jugs," "jobs," etc.).

```
??sk
```

Finds and returns all text containing four-letter words ending with "sk" (e.g., "task," "husk," etc.).

```
t??k
```

Finds and returns all text containing four-letter words beginning with "t" and ending with "k" (e.g., "task," "talk," etc.).

```
fl?sh*ness
```

Finds and returns words such as the following: "flashiness," "fleshiness," "fleshlymindness," etc.

Use All Wildcard Matches

The search option Use All Wildcard Matches will only work if a Global Word List is available to NEBRL. If the Global Word List is available but not up to date, the Use All Wildcard Matches option will work, but the options presented will be limited to the words available in the available Global Word List.

Character Classes

NEBRL searches include the character class capability of setting classes and ranges of characters to be used as patterns for searching. These characters are placed inside square brackets ([ ]).

For example, to search for "Jeremiah" or "Nehemiah" you could type:

```
[JN]e[rh]emiah
```

Either "J" or "N" is allowed before "e[rh]emiah," but not "H." If you had typed "[JNH]e[rhz]e[mk]iah," "Hezekiah" could have been found as well.

The caret (^) or exclamation point (!) may be used to designate NOT.

For example, to search for any word beginning in "Aha," but *not* "Ahab" or "Ahad" you could type:

```
Aha[!bd]
```

Ranges of characters can be specified using the hyphen (-).

For example, to search for any occurrences of dates in the twentieth century in a book you want to find four-digit strings of characters beginning with "19." You could type:

```
19[0-9][0-9]
```

This search will find all dates from 1900 to 1999. The hyphen indicates the range of characters from 0 to 9.

You can search for three character capitalized abbreviations (i.e., IBM, KJV, etc.) the same way:

```
[A-Z][A-Z][A-Z]
```

The exclamation point or caret can be used to exclude classes of characters from the search.

For example, to find all four-letter strings ending in "ook" which may start with anything *but* a lowercase letter you could type:

```
[^a-z]ook
```

This search allows any first character *except* the lowercase letters a through z.

Search Results Window

When a search is in progress, the **Search Results** window appears (Fig. 4-14).

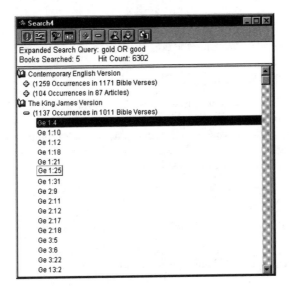

Figure 4-14 Search Results Window.

Following is a description of the Search Results window:

Expanded Search Query

The Expanded Search Query box displays the actual search query as understood by the NEBRL search engine.

For example, enter in the Search Query box the following:

```
go?d
```

If you also uncheck the Use All Wildcard Matches box, the **Choose Wildcard Matches** dialog appears. Click "gold" and "good" as the words to be used in the search. Perform the search. The Expanded Search Query box displays: "gold OR good" (Fig. 4-14) as the actual search command which was performed.

Search Results Toolbar

The Search Results window has its own Toolbar (Fig. 4-14). Many of the features in the Search Results window can be accessed from its Toolbar.

Cancel Search

To cancel a search while it is still in progress, do either of the following:

- Click the **Cancel Search** button 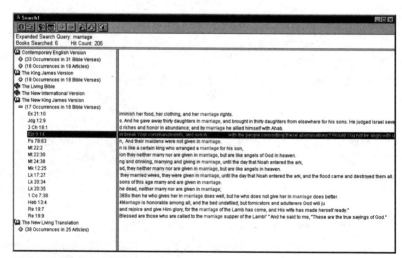 on the Search Results Toolbar.

- Select *Cancel Search* from the **Edit** menu (ALT+E,N) [CTRL+BREAK].

Search Target Window

When a Search Results window is specified as the Search Target window, the results of all future searches will be displayed in this window. In other words, the results of each search will replace those of the previous search in the same window. If you do not select this feature, each search you perform will open a new Search Results window.

To specify a Search Results window as the Search Target window, do either of the following:

- Click the **Search Target Window** button on the Search Results Toolbar.

- Select *Search Target Window* from the **Edit** menu (ALT+E,W).

Show Hits in Context

After a search is performed you can display the hits within the context of the text line in which they occur (Fig. 4-15). You can then quickly scan the contexts of each search hit to locate the hit in which you are most inter-

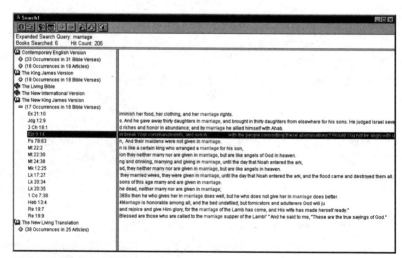

Figure 4-15 Show Hits in Context.

ested. Then display the entire book passage containing the search match. (To display the book passage containing the search match, see **Search Hits Display**.)

To display the search hits in context, do either of the following:

■ Click the **Show Hits in Context** button ▨ on the Search Results Toolbar. The search hits will display in their context.

■ Select *Show Hits in Context* from the **View** menu (ALT+V,X).

> NOTE: Sometimes the article title on the left side of the splitter bar may not clearly identify the location of the search hit in the book. Of course, you can double-click the search hit to open the book to the location of the hit which will enable you to determine if this is a hit in which you are interested. However, when you are scanning down the list of search hits it may be easier and quicker to keep track of where the hits are located in the book by right-clicking on the search hit, opening the right mouse menu, and then clicking *Sync Browser* (⌐ +Y). The Browser will expand and reveal the article location of the hit within the book.

Expand Hit List

After a search is performed, the books which contain search hits will be listed (Fig. 4-16). Beneath the book title will be a title line, with a plus sign (+) in front of it, describing the hits in the list (e.g., "19 Occurrences in 18 Bible Verses"). This list can be expanded to display the list of search hits. To expand the list, first highlight the target list title by clicking on it (Fig. 4-16).

Do either of the following:

■ Click the **Expand Hit List** button ▨ on the Search Results Toolbar to display the individual hits (Fig. 4-17) [RIGHT ARROW].

■ Select *Expand Hit List* from the **View** menu (ALT+V,E) (⌐ +E).

> NOTE: The hit lists in the Search Results window function much like the Library Browser. Expand and shrink the lists by: (1) using the keyboard RIGHT ARROW and LEFT ARROW; (2) clicking on the plus sign next to the list title; or (3) double-clicking on the list titles just as you would in the Library Browser.

Shrink Hit List

After a search is performed, the book titles with search hits will be listed. If you have expanded one of the lists, displaying the individual search hits, and wish to shrink the list so that only its title is displaying, highlight the target list title by clicking on it. The list title line will have a minus sign (–) in front of it. Do either of the following:

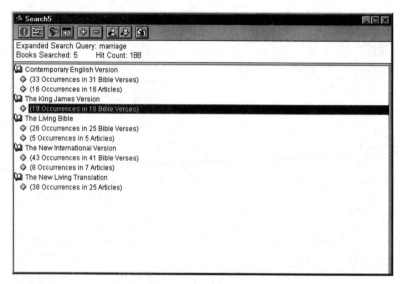

Figure 4-16 Search Hit List Title Selected.

■ Click the **Shrink Hit List** button 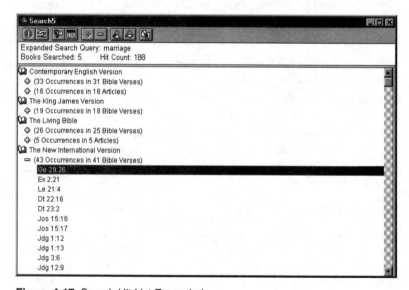 on the Search Results Toolbar to shrink the list so that only its title is displaying (Fig. 4-16).

Figure 4-17 Search Hit List Expanded.

■ Select *Shrink Hit List* from the **View** menu (ALT+V,H) (⌥+R).

NOTE: The hit lists in the Search Results window function much like the Library Browser. Expand and shrink the lists using the keyboard RIGHT ARROW and LEFT ARROW or by double-clicking on the list titles just as you would in the Library Browser. To collapse all entries under a book title, click on the title to highlight it. The book title has an open book 📖 in front of it. Click **Shrink Hit List**, leaving only the book title displaying.

Previous and Next Hit

The Next Search Hit feature jumps to the next search hit in the hit list and jumps to the search hit in the appropriate book.

To jump to the next search hit, do either of the following:

■ Click the **Next Hit** button ▨ on the Search Results Toolbar.

■ Select *Next Search Hit* from the **View** menu (ALT+V,N) [CTRL+DOWN ARROW].

The Previous Search Hit feature jumps to the previous search hit in the hit list as well as jumps to the search hit in the appropriate book.

To jump to the previous search hit, do either of the following:

■ Click the **Previous Hit** button ▨ on the Search Results Toolbar.

■ Select *Previous Search Hit* from the **View** menu (ALT+V,P) [CTRL+UP ARROW].

NOTE: The keystroke commands (CTRL+DOWN ARROW or UP ARROW) will access next and previous search hits while you are working in any book on your screen. In other words, while the Search Results window must remain open on your screen, it need not be the currently active window for this feature to work. For example, you have moved from the Search Results window to the first search hit which is in the KJV Bible. The KJV Bible window is now your active window and you are reading the verse that was found in your search. While the KJV is the active window you may press CTRL+DOWN ARROW to jump to the next search hit. If the next search hit is in a book which is not yet open on your screen, that book will open automatically.

Transfer Hits

Search hits can be transferred to a note file. (See **Transferring Search Hits to Notes** in chapter five, "Notes and Cross References.")

To transfer a search hit or a list of hits to a note file, first highlight the search hit reference by clicking it, or, if you want to transfer all of the hits, highlight the list title. Then, do either of the following:

- Click the **Transfer Hits** button on the Search Results Toolbar.
- Select *Transfer Hit(s) to Note File* from the **Edit** menu (ALT+E,T) [CTRL+T].

Search Hits Display

Below the Expanded Search Query box is the Search Hits list. When a list is expanded (see above), the list of hit references displays (Fig. 4-17). To see the actual hits within context, click the **Show Hits in Context** button. A vertical splitter bar will appear, separating the hit references on the left side of the window from the hits-in-context display on the right side (Fig. 4-15).

The Search Hits list shows all of the Bible references and non-Bible articles which match the search you entered. You may begin to scroll through the list to view all of the references as soon as the list begins to display even though the search is still progressing. (The list will begin to display as soon as NEBRL has completed searching the first book.)

To jump to the location of a hit within a book, do any of the following:

- Double-click on the hit reference on the left side of the Search Results window. The book will open (if it is not already open) and jump to that location.

- With the Search Results dialog the active window (the Title Bar is highlighted), select *Currently Selected Hit* from the **View** menu (ALT+V,U) [ENTER] (⏚+V).

- Click the Next Hit and Previous Hit buttons on the Search Results Toolbar.

- Select *Next Search Hit* and *Previous Search Hit* from the **View** menu (ALT+V,[NP]) [CTRL+DOWN ARROW or UP ARROW].

- Link the Search Results window and the book window by clicking the Link button on each window's Toolbar, opening the Link menu, and selecting the same Link Set for both windows. With the windows linked make the Search Results dialog the active window by clicking on one of the search hits. Now press the DOWN ARROW or UP ARROW to scroll through the hits in the Search Results window. Because the book window is linked to the Search Results window, the book will jump to each hit as you move through them using the arrow keys. Using this method it is not necessary to hold down the CTRL key while using the arrow keys. (See **Linking Books** in chapter three.)

Right Mouse Searching

Many searches can be performed quickly and efficiently using right mouse menus without the necessity of opening the Search dialog. These searches include: Speed searches, KeyLink searches, Topic searches, Reference searches, and Atlas searches.

Speed Search

Speed search is a fast and easy way to perform many concordance and phrase searches. It can bypass the Search dialog and search directly from the active document window.

To perform a Speed search on a *phrase* rather than merely a single word, you must first highlight the search phrase. Select the entire phrase by clicking and dragging the mouse over the text from the beginning of the first word in the phrase to the end of the last to highlight it (Fig. 4-18).

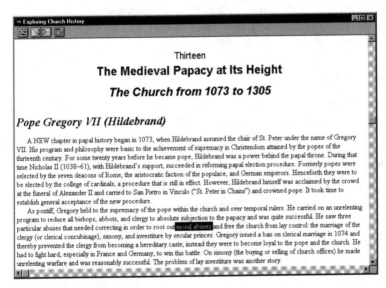

Figure 4-18 Highlighted Phrase.

After highlighting the target phrase, you are ready to perform a Speed search exactly as you would on a single word.

Position the cursor over the target word or phrase. Click the right mouse button. (When performing a concordance Speed search on a single word, it is not necessary to highlight the word before initiating the search. Clicking the right mouse button on a word automatically highlights it.) The right mouse menu will appear. Position the mouse cursor on *Speed Search*. The

Speed Search sub-menu opens. Slide the mouse sideways onto the sub-menu. You have four choices:

- Click *Active Book* (✓⏻+S,A). NEBRL will search for the word or phrase in the active book.

- Click *All Open Books* (✓⏻+S,O). NEBRL will search for the word or phrase in all open books on your screen.

- Click *All Books* (✓⏻+S,B). NEBRL will search for the word or phrase in all books in your library.

- Click *Search Dialog* (✓⏻+S,D). NEBRL will open the main Search dialog with the word or phrase already entered in the Search Query box. Modify the search options as needed.

> **NOTE:** Rather than using the right mouse menu, you can customize the main Toolbar to include a Speed Search button. To initiate a Speed search, highlight a word or phrase by clicking and dragging across it, then click the Speed Search button on the Toolbar. For details on customizing the Toolbar, see **Toolbar** in chapter seven, "System Management."

KeyLink Search

KeyLinks are links between a particular language and the default type of search NEBRL will perform when you select a word in that language. For example, if you select a Greek word in a book, the KeyLink you have preset will determine the default lexicon NEBRL should search and whether you want to perform a Topic search or a full text search.

For each language to be searched using KeyLink, you must define a KeyLink. KeyLinks can be set to search the defined KeyLink book for the selected word by: opening the Topic Browser; performing a Topic search; or performing a full text concordance search.

For more information on defining KeyLinks, see **Languages** in chapter seven, "System Management."

To perform a KeyLink search:

- Click the right mouse button on a word, opening the right mouse menu. Click *KeyLink* (✓⏻+L). The KeyLink search will be performed as defined for the language of the word.

- Double-click on a word. (Double-clicking a word initiates a KeyLink search only if you have set the Double-Click Action option in the General tab panel of the Preferences dialog to initiate a KeyLink Lookup. See **Preferences, General** in chapter seven, "System Management.")

Topic Search

The Topic search is a search for a topic within a book(s). These topics are generally associated with book articles, chapters, or major headings within chapters.

To perform a Topic search:

Click the right mouse button on a word, opening the right mouse menu. Position the mouse cursor on *Topic Search*. The Topic Search sub-menu opens. Slide the mouse sideways onto the sub-menu. You have four choices:

- Click *Active Book* (⌥+T,A). NEBRL will search for the word in the active book.

- Click *All Open Books* (⌥+T,O). NEBRL will search for the word in all open books on your screen.

- Click *All Books* (⌥+T,B). NEBRL will search for the word in all books in your library.

- Click *Search Dialog* (⌥+T,D). NEBRL will open the main Search dialog with the word already entered in the Search Query box and the Search Type set to Topic. Modify the search options as needed.

Instead of using the right mouse menu, you can initiate a Topic search by double-clicking on a word. (Double-clicking a word initiates a Topic search only if you have set the Double-Click Action option in the General tab panel of the Preferences dialog to initiate a Topic search. See **Preferences, General** in chapter seven, "System Management.")

Instead of performing a Topic search, you can open the Topic Browser, from which you can browse the topics and their matching articles in the active book or all books. In this way perhaps you can manually locate information close to your original target.

To open the Topic Browser, do one of the following:

- In the Library Browser select the book whose topics you wish to browse, by clicking on its title, highlighting it. With the highlight bar on the book title, click the right mouse button, opening the right mouse menu. Click *View Topic Browser* (⌥+T) [CTRL+K]. The Topic Browser will open. Type or select a topic. A list of matching articles will appear in the Articles list box. Select the desired article and click the *View Selection* button or double-click on the article title.

   NOTE: You can also initiate a right-mouse-menu Topic Search from the Topic Browser. Since the Topic Browser browses either the book of your choice or all books in your library, probably the two reasons for executing a right-mouse-menu Topic search from the Browser are: (1) The right mouse menu gives you the added option of searching *all open books* rather than *all* books in your library. Therefore, you can easily limit your search to the books which are open on your screen rather than one or all. (2) You can see your hits in context in the Search Results window. This may assist you in more quickly locating appropriate hits.

■ Select *Topic Browser* from the **View** menu (ALT+V,T) [CTRL+K]. Proceed as in the previous method.

NOTE: Rather than using the **View** menu, you can customize the main Toolbar to include a Topic Browser button. To open the Topic Browser, you would then click the **Topic Browser** button on the Toolbar. For details on customizing the Toolbar, see **Toolbar** in chapter seven, "System Management."

Reference Search

The Reference search finds all occurrences of the Bible reference specified (e.g., Exodus 12:37) within a book(s). This is a search for the actual reference, "Exodus 12:37," *not* the text of the verse. NEBRL will locate all occurrences of the reference Exodus 12:37, even if they are spelled "Ex 12:37," "Ex. 12.37," "12.37," "v. 37," etc.

To perform a Reference search:

Click the right mouse button on a Bible reference (e.g., Exodus 12:37), opening the right mouse menu. Position the mouse cursor on *Reference Search*. The Reference Search sub-menu opens. Slide the mouse sideways onto the sub-menu. You have four choices:

■ Click *Active Book* (⌥+R,A). NEBRL will search for the reference in the active book.

■ Click *All Open Books* (⌥+R,O). NEBRL will search for the reference in all open books on your screen.

■ Click *All Books* (⌥+R,B). NEBRL will search for the reference in all books in your library.

■ Click *Search Dialog* (⌥+R,D). NEBRL will open the main Search dialog with the reference search already entered in the Search Query box. Modify the search options as needed.

Instead of performing a Reference search, you can open the Reference Browser, from which you can browse the references and matching articles in the active book. In this way perhaps you can manually locate information close to your original target.

To open the Reference Browser, do one of the following:

■ In the Library Browser select the book whose Bible references you wish to browse, by clicking on its title, highlighting it. With the highlight bar on the book title, click the right mouse button, opening the right mouse menu. Click *View Bible Reference Browser* (⌘+R) [CTRL+R]. The Reference Browser will open. Type or select a Bible reference. A list of matching articles will appear in the Articles list box. Select the desired article and click the *View* button or double-click on the article title.

> NOTE: You can also initiate a right mouse menu Reference Search from the Reference Browser. Since the Reference Browser browses either the book of your choice or all books in your library, probably the only reason for executing a Reference search from the Browser is that the right mouse menu gives you the added option of searching *all open books* rather than *all* books in your library. Therefore, you can easily limit your search to a few select books which are open on your screen rather than one or all. To do this, right-click a reference in the reference list of the Reference Browser, opening the right mouse menu. Click *Search All Open Books*.

■ Select *Bible Reference Browser* from the **View** menu (ALT+V,R) [CTRL+R]. Proceed as in the previous method.

Atlas Search

The Atlas search performs either a Speed search on an Atlas (either Logos Bible Atlas or Parsons Atlas products) or a Reference search on an Atlas (Logos Bible Atlas only).

To perform an Atlas search:

1. Click the right mouse button on a word (Speed search) or a Bible reference (Reference search), opening the right mouse menu.

2. Click *Search Atlas* (ALT+E,L) (⌘+E). NEBRL will start the Atlas program (if it is not already running) and then perform the appropriate search.

> NOTE: The Atlas search requires that you have properly set up your system for Atlas searching in the **Preferences** dialog. (See **DDE** in chapter seven, "System Management.")

Limitations

When searching for phrases, NEBRL searches for phrases *within* Bible verses and non-Bible articles. If you select a phrase that crosses a verse or article boundary, it will not be found.

5

Notes and Cross References

In printed Bibles the translator's notes and cross references normally appear in margins or at the end of verses or paragraphs. Similarly, in non-Bible books footnotes appear at the bottom of the page and endnotes at the end of chapters or book. In NEBRL the text on the screen is not cluttered with this extra information, yet all notes and cross references are readily available for instant display.

There are two types of notes and cross references:

■ Those provided by publishers.

■ Those created by the user.

Publishers' Notes and Cross References

Many books have their own cross reference and note reference schemes designed by the book's publisher. To display publishers' notes and cross references:

■ In most cases the notes and cross references are indicated in the text by **Hot Spots**, highlighted superscript letters, numbers (e.g., ª), or symbols (e.g., *). Positioning the cursor over one of these hot spots will change the cursor to the hand cursor. Click on the hot spot and a popup window appears with the note or cross references. In the case of a note, read it and then click the close button in the upper left corner of the popup window. In the case of cross references, these are **Ref Mark** hot spots. Click a cross reference in the popup window, and a book will go to the reference. (See **Hot Spots** in chapter three, "Viewing a Book.")

■ In some cases notes and/or cross references are provided as a separate book. For example, *The New Treasury of Scripture Knowledge* is a book of over 572,000 cross references provided as a basic text in the NEBRL library. Open the book and go to the Bible verse of your choice, just as you would in a Bible. For each verse you will find cross references. Click a cross reference and a Bible will jump to the reference.

User Notes

NEBRL's Scholar's Notes System enables you to create your own notes and cross references. After you have collected the desired material for a study and have created notes on the material, you can rearrange your notes in any order appropriate to the presentation of the study, including indenting note labels to different levels thereby creating an outlined topical study. This study can be complete with all ancillary material: scripture passages, passages quoted from non-Bible material, user notes, and cross references to additional supporting material.

Creating a Note

A user note is user-created text that is stored in a NEBRL note file. (A NEBRL note file has a .NOT extension.) Usually a note has been attached to a specific location in a book (e.g., Bible verse or book article). Any location in a book may have its own note. Notes attached to Bible verses can be version *independent*. For example, a note attached to Daniel 4:35 in the King James Version can be available in all other Bible versions as well. However, a note attached to a specific word in a Bible version verse is version *specific*. This type of note relates to a specific word occurring in a specific Bible translation.

Notes can be created in either of three ways:

■ Use the **Add a Note** dialog.

■ Use *Add a Note* from the right mouse menu.

■ Make a selection in the active text window and then use any item on the **Default Note Color** menu found on the *Edit* menu.

Using the Add a Note Dialog

Advantages: The advantages to creating a note from the Add a Note dialog are that you can create an "unattached note" (a note attached only to a label), and you do not need to have the book open to the location where you want to attach the note.

Disadvantages: In many cases filling in the Add a Note dialog is slower than using the right mouse menu.

To create a note using the Add a Note dialog:

1. Select the **Add a Note** dialog using any one of the following methods:

   ■ Select *Add a Note* from the **Edit** menu (ALT+E,A).

   ■ Click the **Add a Note** button on the note window toolbar if a note window is already open.

   ■ Right click inside a book window, opening the right mouse menu. Position the cursor over *Add a Note*. A sub-menu opens. Click *Add Note Dialog* (⌥⌘+N,D).

2. A note window will open (if one is not already open), and the **Add a Note** dialog will appear (Fig. 5-1). The Add a Note dialog provides for

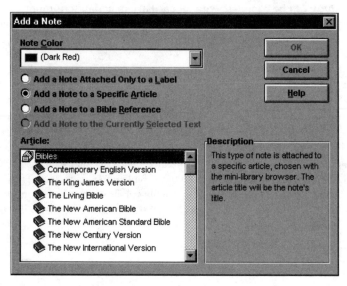

Figure 5-1 Add a Note Dialog.

four types of notes: an unattached note (attached only to a label), a note attached to a Bible reference (version specific or independent); a note attached to a specific article of a book (Bible or non-Bible); and a note attached to the current selection. The Add a Note dialog also allows the user to set the color of the note. To set the color of the note, simply select the desired color (or no color, if that is desired) from the Note Color drop-down list. The default selection in the Note Color drop-down is the current default note color. The default note color can be set at any time using the **Default Note Color** menu found on the **Edit** menu.

3. Click the appropriate button for the type of note desired (in Fig. 5-1 the Article Note button is clicked), then follow the instructions in the Description box:

■ **Unattached Note**: This type of note is not attached to an article or Bible verse, but rather is attached only to a label you assign. Click the Add a Note Attached Only to a Label button. In the Note Label box type the name of this note. For example, this note may be your introductory thoughts on your study of faithfulness. In the box you might type *FAITHFULNESS*. Click *OK*. The label FAITHFULNESS will display in the left side of the note window and you may begin adding your introductory thoughts on faithfulness in the right-hand text side of the note window. In the future, whenever you click on the label FAITHFULNESS in the left side of the window, this note text will display in the right side.

■ **Bible Reference Note**: This type of note is attached to a specific Bible reference which will be the note's label. Click the Add a Note to a Bible Reference button. To specify the reference, type it in the Reference box. To make the note version-specific, check Version Specific and then select the desired Bible version. Click *OK*. The Bible reference label will display in the left side of the note window and you may begin adding your note text in the right-hand text side of the note window. In the future, whenever you click on the reference label in the left side of the window, this note text will display in the right side.

■ **Article Note**: This type of note is attached to a specific article, chosen with the mini-library browser in this dialog. The article title will be the note's label. Click the Add a Note to a Specific Article button. To specify the article, scroll down the Article list and select the desired article title, just as you would select an article to open in the regular Library Browser. Click *OK*. The article title label will display in the left side of the note window and you may begin adding your note text in the right-hand text side of the note window. In the future, whenever you click on the article label in the left side of the window, this note text will display in the right side.

■ **Selection Note**: This type of note is attached to the selection in the current text window. If the book is a versified book, such as a Bible or a commentary, the note label will be the verse in which the selection was made. If the book is any other type of book, the note label will be the title of the current article. To add this type of note, first make a selection in the text window. Then select Add a Note from the Edit menu and click on the radio button entitled "Add a Note to the currently selected text." Next, click OK to add the note.

Using the Right Mouse Menu

Advantages: The advantages to creating a note from the right mouse menu, bypassing the Add a Note dialog, are that you can attach the note to a specific word or phrase in the text if you desire, and in many cases using the right mouse menu is quicker than filling in the Add a Note dialog.

Disadvantages: The disadvantages are that you cannot create an "unattached note" (a note attached only to a label), and you must have the book open to the location where you want to attach the note.

To create a note using the right mouse menu:

1. Select the text location in the book (Bible or non-Bible) where you want the note marker 🖰 to appear:

- Note attached to the *beginning* of an article or Bible verse. Go to step 2.

- Note attached to a *specific word or phrase* in an article or Bible verse. Go to step 4.

2. **Attached to beginning of article or Bible verse.** Right click anywhere in the article or Bible verse to which you want to attach a note. The right mouse menu appears. Position the cursor over *Add a Note.* A sub-menu opens.

3. Click "To Verse," "To Verse and Bible," or "To Article" to attach a note to the beginning of a Bible verse, a version-specific verse, or a Bible chapter, respectively (⌐☐+N,[V,B,A]). Click "To Article" to attach a note to the beginning of a non-Bible article. (In non-Bibles "To Verse" and "To Verse and Bible" are not available options.) A Note Marker will appear at the beginning of the article or verse and a note window will open with the blinking insertion cursor waiting for you to insert text.

4. **Attached to a specific word.** To attach a note to the word "sluggard" in the KJV version of Proverbs 6:6, open the KJV Bible to Proverbs 6:6 and right-click the mouse on the word "sluggard." The word becomes highlighted and the right mouse menu opens. Position the cursor over *Add a Note* (⌐☐+N). A sub-menu opens. Go to step 6.

5. **Attached to a specific phrase.** Position the mouse cursor at the beginning of the phrase in the text where you want the note attached. To attach a note to the phrase "Go to the ant" position the cursor on the "G" and then click and drag the mouse from left to right to the comma after "ant," selecting the entire phrase. Release the left mouse button and the phrase remains highlighted (Fig. 5-2). Position the cursor *anywhere over*

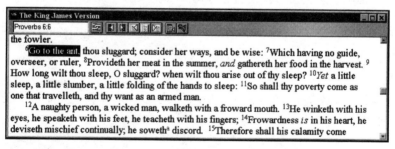

Figure 5-2 Click and Drag Phrase Selection.

the highlighted phrase and click the right mouse button. (It is important that the cursor be positioned over the highlighted phrase when you click the right mouse button so NEBRL knows that the right mouse selection will apply to the highlighted word.) The right mouse menu opens. Position the cursor over *Add a Note* (⌥+N). A sub-menu opens. Go to step 6.

6. Click "To Selection" (⌥+N,S). A Note Marker appears at the end of the phrase you selected (Fig. 5-3), and a note window opens with the blink-

> **⁶Go to the ant, 📋 thou sluggard;**

Figure 5-3 Note Marker.

ing insertion cursor waiting for you to insert text. Note that in Bibles the note label will be version-specific because you selected a particular word or phrase in a Bible version, so the label will read, "KJV: Pr 6:6."

Using the Default Note Color Menu

Advantages: You can quickly create a note with the desired color without having to first add the note and then selecting the color and without having to use the Add a Note dialog.

Disadvantages: You can only create notes on the current selection using this method.

To create a note using the **Default Note Color** menu:

1. Select the text location in the book (Bible or non-Bible) where you want the note marker 📋 to appear.

2. Go to the **Default Note Color** menu, found on the **Edit** menu. Select the desired color from this menu. Select *No Color* if you don't want the note to have a color. You can also use the Default Note Color toolbar button

   on the main toolbar. If this button isn't available, you can add it by customizing the toolbar.

This Note Marker will always appear in the text if two conditions are true:

■ You have not deleted the note from the note file.

■ The note file in which the note exists is open. You may create multiple note files, each with a different set of notes. The file which contains the note for Proverbs 6:6 "Go to the ant," must be open in order for the Note Marker to appear next to "ant."

Adding Text to a Note

There are many ways you can insert text into your notes:

■ Type your desired text in the note window.

- Select text in other NEBRL books or your favorite Windows word processor (by clicking and dragging with the left mouse button over the text to highlight it), copy it to the Windows clipboard, and then paste it into your note. (See **Working with Word Processors** in chapter six, "Printing, Exporting, Importing, and Word Processors.")

- Select the text in other NEBRL books (click and drag the left mouse button over the text to highlight it). Left-click and hold down the mouse button on the highlighted block of text and drag it into the note window. The text block will be inserted where the blinking cursor is positioned in the note.

  NOTE: Bibliographic citations may be appended to any text inserted into your notes or copied to the Windows Clipboard. (See **Citations** in chapter seven, "System Management.")

Creating a New Note File

User notes and cross references are both saved in NEBRL note files (files with the .NOT extension). Every time you create a new NEBRL note file, you can create a new set of notes and cross references which may be recalled at any time by opening the appropriate note file. In other words, for each subject you study, you can create a new note file with a new set of applicable notes and cross references.

To create a new note file when no other note files are open:

1. Ensure that there are no other note files currently open.

2. Create a new note, and a new note file will be created automatically. (If other note files are open, creating a new note will insert the note into the most recently active note window rather than creating a new note file.)

To create a new note file while other note files are open:

1. Do either of the following:

   - Select *New* from the **File** menu (ALT+F,N) [CTRL+N].

   - Click the **File New** button ![File New button] on the main Toolbar.

   The default main Toolbar does not have the File New button. You can add this button to the main Toolbar if you desire. To add the button, you must customize the Toolbar. See **Toolbar** in chapter seven, "System Management."

Modifying a Note

NEBRL provides basic text formatting features.

To change the formatting for text as you type, select the appropriate formatting option, then continue typing. The new text will be in the new format.

To change the formatting of existing text, click and drag the left mouse button over the desired text to select and highlight it. Then apply any of the following formatting options.

Bold

To change note text to **bold**, do any of the following:

- Click the **Bold** button ▣ on the note window Toolbar.
- Select *Bold* from the **Format** menu (ALT+R,B) [CTRL+B] (⌘+B).

    NOTE: The Format menu only exists when the note window is active because the only text you are allowed to format is your own note text.

Italic

To change note text to *italic*, do any of the following:

- Click the **Italic** button ▣ on the note window Toolbar.
- Select *Italic* from the **Format** menu (ALT+R,I) [CTRL+I] (⌘+I).

    NOTE: The Format menu only exists when the note window is active because the only text you are allowed to format is your own note text.

Language

To change the language of note text:

1. Do any of the following:

    - Click the **Language** button ▣ on the note window Toolbar.
    - Select *Language* from the **Format** menu (ALT+R,L) [CTRL+L] (⌘+L).

2. Select the desired language from the list box. Click *OK*. The language will automatically change to the font appropriate for the language. (See **Languages** in chapter seven, "System Management.")

    NOTE: The Format menu only exists when the note window is active because the only text you are allowed to format is your own note text.

Font

To change note text font and size:

1. Select *Font* from the **Format** menu (ALT+R,F) (⌘+F).

2. Select a font and a font size from the list boxes. Click *OK*.

NOTE: The Format menu only exists when the note window is active because the only text you are allowed to format is your own note text.

Plain

To change note text from bold and/or italic back to plain format (discontinue bold and/or italic formatting), do any of the following:

■ Select *Plain* from the **Format** menu (ALT+R,P) (⌥⌘+P).

■ When bold is selected, selecting bold again will unselect it. The same is true for italics.

NOTE: The Format menu only exists when the note window is active because the only text you are allowed to format is your own note text.

Delete

To delete note text:

1. Click and drag the left mouse button over the target text to select and highlight it.

2. Delete the text by doing either of the following:

■ Press the keyboard DELETE key.

■ Select *Clear* from the right mouse menu (⌥⌘+Clear).

Transferring Search Hits to Notes

NEBRL allows you to transfer search hits into your note file as note labels.

The effect is that of creating a topical index. Search for all of the references in your books which relate to a particular word or topic, then use that list of references as labels to which you attach your notes. With this list of note labels in your note file, you can jump to each search hit relating to the topic and write notes on it.

To transfer search hits into your note file, do the following:

1. After you have performed a search, the Search Results dialog is displayed. Decide whether you want to transfer all of the search results or only selected references. You can transfer search hits one at a time to the note file or you can transfer all of the hits as a group. If you have a large group of search hits and you want to transfer most of them, it is quicker to transfer all of them and then, in the note window, delete the few you don't want.

2. To transfer an individual search hit, click it to select it (Fig. 5-4).

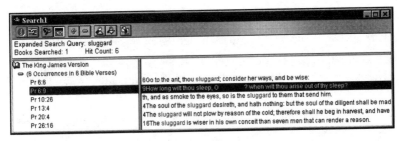

Figure 5-4 Selecting a Search Hit for Transfer to Note File.

3. To transfer the entire list, click the title line above the list (Fig. 5-5).

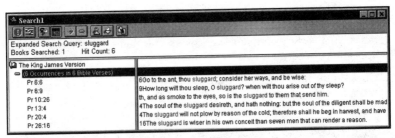

Figure 5-5 Selecting all Search Hits for Transfer to Note File.

4. Do any of the following:

   ■ Click the **Transfer Hits** button on the Search Results Toolbar.

   ■ Select *Transfer Hits to Note File* from the **Edit** menu (ALT+E,T)
     [CTRL+T] (⌘+T).

5. The search hit appears as a note label in the left side of the note window
   (Fig. 5-6). Jump to the search hit by double-clicking the note label. The
   note itself is empty and ready for your input.

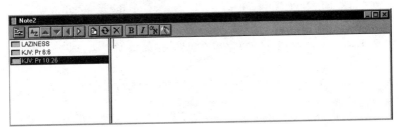

Figure 5-6 Search Hit Transferred as a Note Label.

Arranging Notes

There are two things you can do to change the arrangement of your notes:

- Reorder the position of your notes in the file. After you have collected information and made notes on it, reorder the information to suit the purpose of your study.

- Create different indent levels for the note labels so as to organize them into an outline.

To reorder the position of your notes in the file:

1. Ensure that the **Notes in Sorted Order** button ![Az button] on the note window Toolbar is not selected (ALT+V,E). If this button is selected, their order cannot be changed.

   NOTE: The **Notes in Sorted Order** button sorts your notes according to the following scheme: (1) all unattached notes; (2) all nonversion-specific notes; (3) all article and verse version-specific notes in the order of their appearance in books.

2. Click on the note label you want to move up or down in the list on the left side of the window, selecting it (Fig. 5-7).

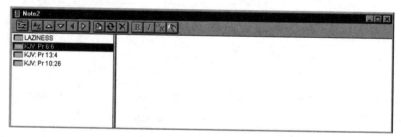

Figure 5-7 Selected Note Label.

3. To move the note label down, do either of the following:

   - Click the **Move Note Down** button ![down button] on the note window Toolbar.

   - Select *Move Note Down* from the **Edit** menu (ALT+E,D) [CTRL+DOWN ARROW].

4. To move the note label up, do either of the following:

   - Click the **Move Note Up** button ![up button] on the note window Toolbar.

   - Select *Move Note Up* from the **Edit** menu (ALT+E,M) [CTRL+UP ARROW].

To create different indent levels for the note labels:

1. Click on the note label you want to indent in the list on the left side of the window, highlighting it.

2. To indent the note label, do either of the following:

   ■ Click the **Indent Note** button on the note window Toolbar.

   ■ Select *Indent Note* from the **Edit** menu (ALT+E,N) [CTRL+RIGHT ARROW].

3. To outdent the note label, do either of the following:

   ■ Click the **Outdent Note** button on the note window Toolbar.

   ■ Select *Outdent Note* from the **Edit** menu (ALT+E,O) [CTRL+LEFT ARROW].

Editing Note Labels

When creating colored notes it is often useful to label each color in use with a word or phrase denoting what the color means. This can be achieved using the Edit Note Labels dialog. When editing a note file, you can open this dialog by selecting Note Labels on the Edit menu.

To change a note label for one or more colors, do the following:

■ Click on a color in the Palette list for which you want a label.

■ Type the desired label in the Label edit control. You can change languages by clicking on the Languages button to the right of the control and selecting a different language.

■ Click on the Close button when done.

Each note file can have its own labels for different colors.

Saving Note Files

When you close either a note window or NEBRL, if you have made any changes to the notes since you opened the file, you will automatically be asked if you want to save the changes to the note file. There are two possibilities:

■ If the file already has a name, click *Yes* and the file is saved.

■ If the file is a new file, as yet unnamed, click *Yes* and the **File Save As** dialog will appear. Choose the drive and directory. Specify a file name in the File Name box. File names follow the standard DOS naming conventions (i.e., eight or fewer characters for the name, followed by a period and a three-character extension). For note files NEBRL automatically supplies the .NOT extension; you need only type the name using eight or fewer characters. For example, entering "faith" will create a file named "faith.not" in the directory selected. If you select a file which already exists in the File Name list box, you will be prompted as to whether you want to overwrite this already-existing file. Click **OK** to overwrite the existing file with your currently selected note file. Otherwise, choose a new file name. When you have the correct file name, click **OK**.

To prevent loss of your data due to power failures, you may want to periodically save your open note file without closing it. Some people ask, "How often should I save my note file?" The answer is, "How many hours of work are you willing to risk losing?" It is probably wise to save your work every five to ten minutes.

To save the current note file while keeping it open:

1. Make the note window the active document window by clicking anywhere inside it, highlighting its title bar.

2. There are two possibilities:

   ■ If the file already has a name, click the **File Save** button on the main Toolbar, or select *Save* from the **File** menu (ALT+F,S) [CTRL+S]. The file is saved, including all changes made since the last time it was saved.

   The default main Toolbar does not have the File Save button. You can add this button to the main Toolbar if you desire. To add the button, you must customize the Toolbar. See **Toolbar** in chapter seven, "System Management."

   ■ If the file is a new file, as yet unnamed, select *Save As* from the **File** menu (ALT+F,A). The **File Save As** dialog will appear. Specify a file name in the File Name box. File names follow the standard DOS naming conventions (i.e., eight or fewer characters for the name, followed by a period and a three-character extension). For note files NEBRL automatically supplies the .NOT extension; you need only type the name using eight or fewer characters. Choose the drive and directory if desired. Click **OK**. Now that the file has a name, the next time you want to save it, all you need to do is click the File Save button on the Toolbar or type CTRL+S (see previous method).

Opening Note Files

To open an existing note file:

1. Do either of the following:

   ■ Click the **File Open** button on the main Toolbar.

The default main Toolbar does not have the File Open button. You can add this button to the main Toolbar if you desire. To add the button, you must customize the Toolbar. See **Toolbar** in chapter seven, "System Management."

■ Select *Open* from the **File** menu (ALT+F,O) [CTRL+O]. The **File Open** dialog appears (Fig. 5-8).

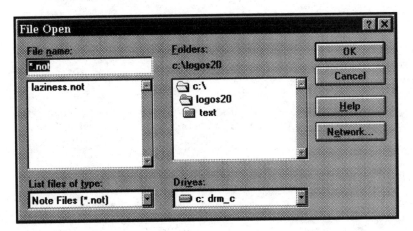

Figure 5-8 File Open Dialog.

2. The file type is preselected for you by NEBRL since all note files have a .NOT extension.

3. Choose the Drive and Directory.

4. Select the desired file in the File Name list box either by double-clicking it or by single-clicking it and then clicking *OK*.

You may have multiple note files open simultaneously. If all of the notes you want are not in a single file, open another file. Move from one file to the other by clicking in each one to make it the active note file, or select the appropriate note file from the **Window** menu.

Viewing Notes

To view a user note:

1. Ensure that the note file containing the desired notes is open. NEBRL is aware of notes, placing Note Markers in the text indicating their presence, only when the appropriate note file is open. This fact allows you to create multiple notes for the same text location. Therefore, opening different note files determines which note is attached to a particular text location.

2. Click the Note Marker 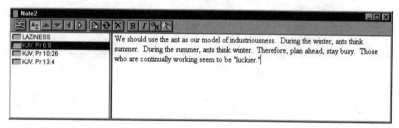 in the text (Fig. 5-9). The note window will jump to the desired note.

⁶Go to the ant, ❧thou sluggard;

Figure 5-9 Clicking the Note Marker.

Viewing Corresponding Text

To view the text which corresponds to a note:

■ In a note window double-click the note label on the left side of the window (Fig. 5-10). The book will jump to the referenced text location. If the text to which the note is attached is not currently open in a document window, NEBRL will open the book and it will jump to the location.

Figure 5-10 Double-clicking the Note Label.

Transferring Notes to Other Note Files

To transfer a note from one note file to another:

1. Ensure that both note files are open. Arrange them on your screen so that the note label panel of each note window is visible (Fig. 5-11).

2. Click the note label of the note you want to transfer, selecting and highlighting it (Fig. 5-11).

3. Click and drag the highlighted note label with the left mouse button to the note label panel of the target note window (Fig. 5-12). The note text will transfer to the other note window along with the label.

Deleting a Note

To delete an existing note from a note window, first select the note by clicking on its label on the left side of the window, highlighting it. Then do either of the following:

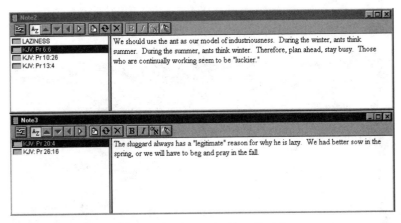

Figure 5-11 Arrange Two Note Windows for Note Transfer.

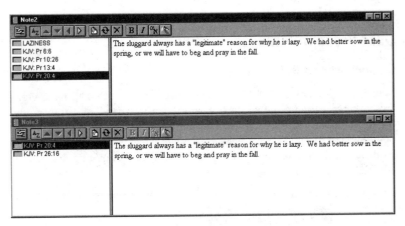

Figure 5-12 Note on Proverbs 20:4 Transferred to Other Note File.

- Click the **Delete Note** button on the note window Toolbar.
- Select *Delete Note* from the **Edit** menu on the main Toolbar (ALT+E,E).

Choosing a Note File

If you attempt to add a note while you have more than one note file open, NEBRL will prompt you for which note file to add the note to.

To choose the note file to add your note to:

■ Select the note file from the list (Fig. 5-12a). Click OK and continue to add your note using the **Add a Note Dialog.**

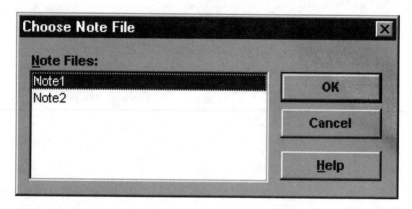

Figure 5-12a Choosing a Note File.

User Cross References

Creating a Cross Reference

A user cross reference is a user-created **hot spot** in note text. Bible verse cross references can be either version specific or independent. For example, a cross reference to Proverbs 6:6 can jump to Proverbs 6:6 in either any open Bible or in a specific Bible selected when the cross reference is created. Non-Bible cross references can jump either to a chapter or an article within a book, or to a specific location within a book.

Cross references are added using the **Add Cross Reference** dialog (Fig. 5-13).

Bible Verse Cross References

To add a new Bible verse cross reference to note text:

1. Position the cursor at the location in the note text where you want to insert the cross reference.

2. Do either of the following:

   ■ Click the **Add Cross Reference** button ![toolbar button] on the note window Toolbar.

   ■ Select *Add Cross Reference* from the **Edit** menu (ALT+E,F) [CTRL+SHIFT+R].

3. Click on the Reference a Bible Verse radio button to add a Bible cross reference. There are two kinds of Bible cross references: Version-specific and Non-version-specific.

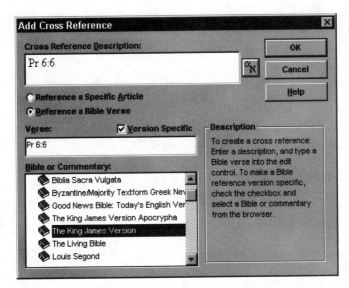

Figure 5-13 Add Cross Reference Dialog.

- To make a version-specific Bible cross reference, click on the Version Specific check box. Next, type the Bible verse in the Reference edit control or select a verse from a Bible or commentary in the Bible or Commentary list.

- To make a non-version-specific Bible cross reference, either type in the Bible verse in the Reference edit control and select a book in the Bible or Commentary list, or simply select a section within a book in the Bible or Commentary list.

4. To make a Bible cross reference version specific, click the checkbox and select a Bible version (e.g., KJV) from the browser on the left (Fig. 5-13).

5. To change the cross reference description from the default description, type a new one in the Cross Reference Description edit control. Note that you can use any language listed in the language dialog by clicking on the Language button ![button] and selecting the desired language.

6. Click **OK**. Your cross reference is entered into the note text as a Reference hot spot (Fig. 5-14).

Non-Bible Article Cross References

To add a new non-Bible article cross reference to note text:

1. Position the cursor at the location in the note text where you want to insert the cross reference.

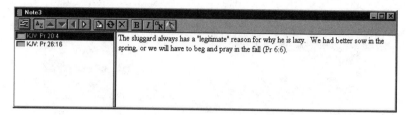

Figure 5-14 Highlighted Cross Reference (Pr 6:6) in Note Text.

2. Do either of the following:

- Click the **Add Cross Reference** button on the note window Toolbar.

- Select *Add Cross Reference* from the **Edit** menu (ALT+E,F) [CTRL+ SHIFT+R].

3. The Add Cross Reference dialog opens. Choose a book or section within a book from the *Article or Book* list. The *Cross Reference Description* control will display the text that will appear in the note text as your cross reference hot spot.

4. To change the cross reference description from the default description, type a new one in the Cross Reference Description edit control. Note that you can use any language listed in the language dialog by clicking

on the Language button and selecting the desired language.

5. Click *OK*. Your cross reference is entered into the note text as a hot spot.

Converting Search Hits to Cross References

To convert a search hit to a cross reference in a note:

1. Ensure that the note file is open. Arrange the Search Results window and the note window on your screen so that the search hit references and the note text are both visible (Fig. 5-15).

2. Click the search hit reference you want to convert into a cross reference, selecting and highlighting it (Fig. 5-15).

3. Click and drag the highlighted reference with the left mouse button to the position in the note text where you want the cross reference. The reference is inserted into the note text as a cross reference hot spot. Clicking on the hot spot causes the appropriate book to jump to that reference.

Jumping to a Cross Reference

NEBRL cross references enable you to jump back and forth between your notes and specific locations in your books.

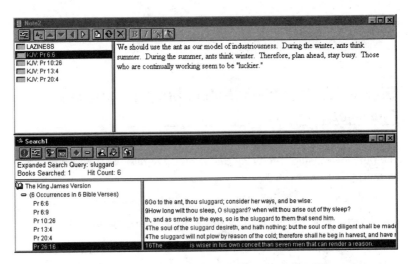

Figure 5-15 Arrange Note and Search Windows for Note Transfer.

Example: You have Proverbs 20:4 displayed in the active document window, and your note for Proverbs 20:4 is displayed in the note window. Proverbs 6:6 is a cross reference appearing in your note on Proverbs 20:4.

To jump to Proverbs 6:6:

■ Click the left mouse button on the cross reference hot spot, Proverbs 6:6. A Bible will jump to Proverbs 6:6.

To return to Proverbs 20:4: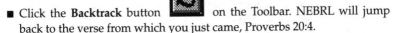

■ Click the **Backtrack** button   on the Toolbar. NEBRL will jump back to the verse from which you just came, Proverbs 20:4.

If you plan to jump from verse to verse using cross references and you want to be able to easily return to your starting verse, set a Bookmark at that verse before you begin. (See **Bookmarks** in chapter three, "Viewing a Book.")

Deleting a Cross Reference

To delete a cross reference from a note:

1. Click and drag the left mouse button over the cross reference to select and highlight it. (You must begin by positioning the cursor on the extreme left side of the cross reference so that the hand cursor changes to the I-beam cursor before you can begin clicking and dragging to select it.)

2. Delete the selected cross reference in either of the following ways:

- Press the keyboard DELETE key.

- Select *Clear* from the right mouse menu (⌐🖰 +Clear).

Organizing Your Work: Notes, Cross References, and Search

Once you have learned how to use many of the powerful NEBRL features, the next logical step is to bring this knowledge into focus in order to best organize research.

We will describe the general steps recommended for efficient study:

1. Select a topic you are going to study, for example, "faithfulness."

2. Open a new note file for this study.

3. Collect information on your topic by searching through your library for whatever words, phrases, and/or topics you feel will best help you study "faith."

4. After each search, transfer the search results to your note file. Each set of search hits you transfer will add to the overall list of labels in the note file.

5. As you study, you may add individual notes to your note file using the Add a Note feature. Add additional cross references to the text of your notes as needed.

6. Turn off "Notes in Sorted Order" in the note window Toolbar. As you develop your thoughts into an outline, reposition the notes in the note window using the **Move Note Up, Move Note Down, Indent Note,** and **Outdent Note** buttons.

7. Add unattached notes to fill out the outline as needed.

8. Delete unwanted note labels from the note window.

9. Save your note file, naming it something like: FAITH.NOT.

10. Finally, print or export your note file, including supporting texts and cross references.

6

Printing, Exporting, Importing, Word Processors

Printing

The Print option allows you to print reports containing:

- A range of Bible verses from any Bible version in your library, complete with translator's notes, if desired.

- Text from any book in your library.

- Search results, with entire text of articles containing hits, if desired.

- Your notes, complete with note labels and referenced text, if desired.

The Print dialog allows you to specify various printing options. The available options differ slightly depending on whether you are printing Bible text, non-Bible text, search results, or a note file.

Access the Print dialog in any of the following ways:

- Click the **Print** button on the main Toolbar.

- Select *Print* from the **File** menu (ALT+F,P) [CTRL+P] (+P).

The Print dialog opens (Fig. 6-1). The Print dialog consists of three tab panels: Print, Format, and Margins, and also the *Print Setup* button. The *Print Setup* button allows you to setup and/or select your printer. See your Windows and printer documentation for information about setting up your printer if you have not already done so.

Print

The Print tab panel takes on three different forms depending on what you are printing: Bible or non-Bible text, search results, or notes.

Print Text

If the current active window is any window other than the Search Results window or a note window when you open the Print dialog, the Print tab panel will provide options for printing Bible or non-Bible text (Fig. 6-1).

You may choose either of the following two options:

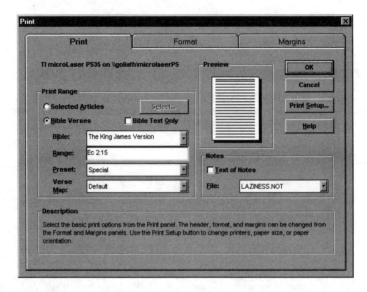

Figure 6-1 Print Dialog: Printing Text.

■ **Selected Articles:** Print selected articles from any of your books. Click *Select* to open the **Range Selection** dialog (Fig. 6-2). Use the Available Items browser on the left to select books, chapters, articles to print. Click the item you want to print, then click and drag it over to the Selected Items list box, click *Add* to move it there, or right-click to open the right

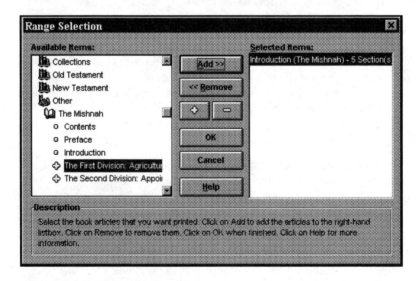

Figure 6-2 Print Range Dialog.

mouse menu and click *Add Item* (‸⊟+A). If you decide to remove an item from the Selected Items list box, click it, then click *Remove* (‸⊟+R). Click *OK* when you are finished selecting items to print.

- **Bible Verses:** Print a range of Bible verses from a particular Bible version. From the drop-down list boxes select the Bible version and either a preset range of Bible books, or a special range of verses. If you do not select the Bible Text Only check box, Bible text plus any supplemental translator's notes will print.

To print any notes which are tied to the print text:

- Click the Text of Notes box and select the appropriate note file from the drop-down list box. (The list box displays the names of note files which are currently open. If the note file you want is not listed, close the Print dialog, open the note file, and then reopen the Print dialog.)

Print Search Results

If the Search Results window is the active window when you open the Print dialog, the Print tab panel will provide options for printing your search results (Fig. 6-3).

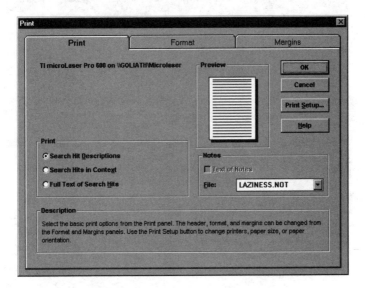

Figure 6-3 Printing Search Results.

You may choose one of the following three options:

- **Search Hit Descriptions:** Print only the descriptions of the search hit locations (for Bibles, this would be the Bible reference, e.g., Gen. 1:1). The search hit descriptions are listed on the left side of the Search Results window.

- **Search Hits in Context:** Print the search hits in context line of text which appears on the right side of the Search Results window when you select Show Search Hits in Context.

- **Full Text of Search Hits:** Print the complete article containing the search hit.

To print any notes which are tied to the search hit references:

- Click the Text of Notes box and select the appropriate note file from the drop-down list box. (The list box displays the names of note files which are currently open. If the note file you want is not listed, close the Print dialog, open the note file, and then reopen the Print dialog.)

Print Notes

If a note window is the active window when you open the Print dialog, the Print tab panel will provide options for printing your notes (Fig. 6-4).

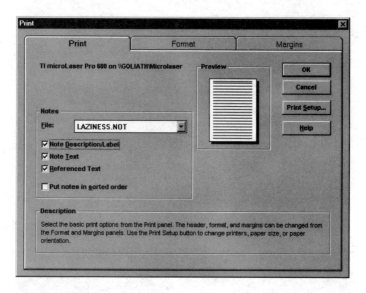

Figure 6-4 Printing Notes.

First, select the note file you want to print from the drop-down list box. The note file you had open when you entered the Print dialog will display in the list box, however you may switch to a different note file if it is also open on the screen. If the note file you want is not listed, close the Print dialog, open the note file, and then reopen the Print dialog.

You may choose any or all of the following four options:

- **Note Description/Label:** Print the note label (found on the left side of the Notes window), which indicates the location to which the note is tied.

- **Note Text:** Print the text of the note.

- **Referenced Text:** Print the book text to which the note is tied. This text is referenced by the note label. For example, if the note label is "Psalm 22:1," this option will print the text of Psalm 22:1.

- **Put notes in sorted order:** If you select this option, the system will ignore your note arrangement and will print the notes in the browser sorted order.

Format

The Format tab panel provides options for the overall appearance of the text of your print document (Fig. 6-5).

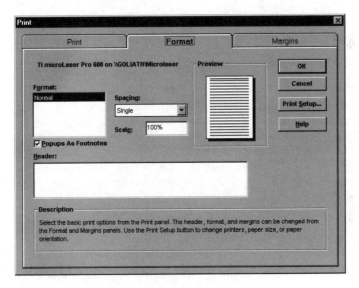

Figure 6-5 Print Dialog: Format Tab Panel.

- **Spacing:** From the drop-down list box select single, double, or triple spacing for the text.

- **Scale:** Select larger or smaller text size by changing the value.

- **Header:** Optionally enter text in this box to appear centered at the top of each page.

Margins

The Margins tab panel provides options for the spacing and column appearance of your print document (Fig. 6-6).

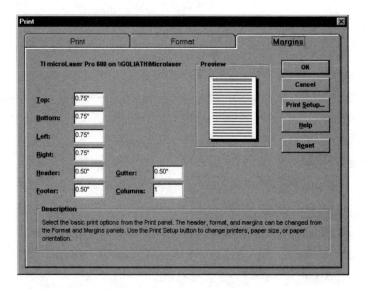

Figure 6-6 Print Dialog: Margins Tab Panel.

The options on the left (Top, Bottom, etc.) affect the margins around the perimeter of the page including below and above the headers and footers. The Gutter option is only operative when you change Columns to a number greater than 1. As you make changes to these options, watch the Preview page in the dialog to see the effect your changes make. All dimensions are in inches.

Exporting

The Export option allows you to export data from NEBRL to four different file formats:

■ ASCII text.

■ Unicode text.

■ Rich Text Format (RTF) (which contains formatted text information).

■ HTML text (HyperText Markup Language), the file format used to structure documents on the World Wide Web and to hyperlink them to other documents, sounds, videos, and images.

NOTE: Rich Text Format (RTF) is an export format which can be used to prepare data for use in a word processor that supports this format. Some word processors may not be able to take advantage of all RTF formatting.

These files can contain:

- A range of Bible verses from any Bible version in your library, complete with translator's notes, if desired.

- Text from any book in your library.

- Search results, with entire text of articles containing hits, if desired.

- Your notes, complete with note labels and referenced text, if desired.

Access the Export dialog as follows:

- Select *Export* from the **File** menu (ALT+F,E).

The Export dialog opens (Fig. 6-7).

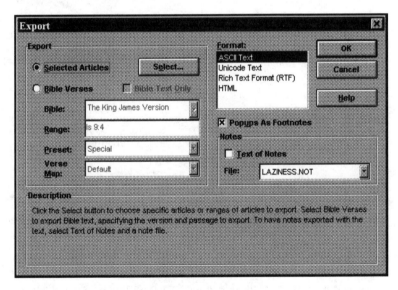

Figure 6-7 Export Dialog: Exporting Text.

The Export dialog takes on three different forms depending on what you are exporting: Bible or non-Bible text, search results, or notes.

Exporting Text

If the current active window is any window other than the Search Results window or a note window when you open the Export dialog, it will provide options for exporting Bible or non-Bible text (Fig. 6-7).

You may choose either of the following two options:

■ **Selected Articles:** Export selected articles from any of your books. Click *Select* to open the **Range Selection** dialog. Use the Available Items browser on the left to select books, chapters, articles to export. Click the item you want to export, then click and drag it over to the Selected Items list box, click *Add* to move it there, or right-click to open the right mouse menu and click *Add Item* (⁀❂+A). If you decide to remove an item from the Selected Items list box, click it, then click *Remove* (⁀❂+R). Click *OK* when you are finished selecting items to export.

■ **Bible Verses:** Export a range of Bible verses from a particular Bible version. From the drop-down list boxes select the Bible version and either a preset range of Bible books, or a special range of verses. If you do not select the Bible Text Only check box, Bible text plus any supplemental translator's notes will export.

To export any notes which are tied to the export text:

■ Click the Text of Notes box and select the appropriate note file from the drop-down list box. (The list box displays the names of note files which are currently open. If the note file you want is not listed, close the Export dialog, open the note file, and then reopen the Export dialog.)

Exporting Search Results

If the Search Results window is the active window when you open the Export dialog, it will provide options for exporting your search results (Fig. 6-8).

You may choose one of the following three options:

■ **Search Hit Descriptions:** Export only the descriptions of the search hit locations (for Bibles, this would be the Bible reference, e.g., Gen. 1:1). The search hit descriptions are listed on the left side of the Search Results window.

■ **Search Hits in Context:** Export the search-hits-in-context line of text which appears on the right side of the Search Results window when you select Show Search Hits in Context.

■ **Full Text of Search Hits:** Export the complete article containing the search hit.

To export any notes which are tied to the search hit references:

■ Click the Text of Notes box and select the appropriate note file from the drop-down list box. (The list box displays the names of note files which are currently open. If the note file you want is not listed, close the Export dialog, open the note file, and then reopen the Export dialog.)

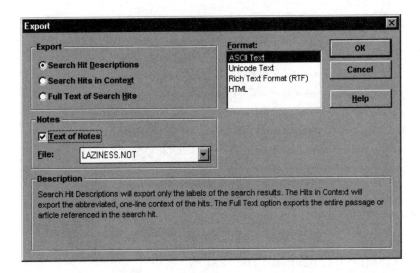

Figure 6-8 Exporting Search Results.

Exporting Notes

If a note window is the active window when you open the Export dialog, it will provide options for exporting your notes (Fig. 6-9).

First, select the note file you want to export from the drop-down list box. The note file you had open when you entered the Export dialog will dis-

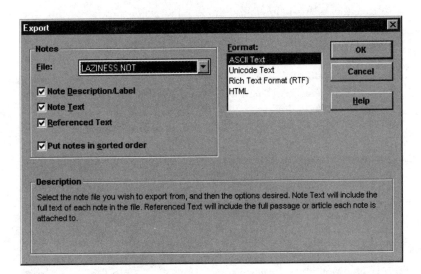

Figure 6-9 Exporting Notes.

play in the list box, however you may switch to a different note file if it is also open on the screen. If the note file you want is not listed, close the Export dialog, open the note file, and then reopen the Export dialog.

You may choose any or all of the following four options:

- **Note Description/Label:** Export the note label (found on the left side of the Notes window), which indicates the location to which the note is tied.

- **Note Text:** Export the text of the note.

- **Referenced Text:** Export the book text to which the note is tied. This text is referenced by the note label. For example, if the note label is "Psalm 22:1," this option will export the text of Psalm 22:1.

- **Put notes in sorted order:** If you select this option, the system will ignore your note arrangement and will export the notes in the browser sorted order.

Working with Word Processors

NEBRL provides four different methods of communicating with popular word processors:

- Export files containing Bible and non-Bible text, search results, and user notes and cross references. These files can then be imported into your word processor in the same manner that you would import other text files. Because the files exported by NEBRL are standard ASCII text files or RTF files, they can be imported into any word processor that accepts ASCII or RTF files. (See **Exporting** in this chapter.)

- Copy either of the following to the Windows clipboard for pasting into NEBRL notes or Windows word processors: (1) selected text fragments, or (2) complete verses, articles, search results, notes. (See **Copy Special and Copy** in this chapter.)

- From inside NEBRL you can insert Bible verses by means of an exclusive NEBRL feature called Dynamic Verse Insertion (DVI). Unlike the previous two methods, this method for inserting Bible verses into a word processor requires the word processor to be a Windows-based application. See **DVI** in this chapter.

- From inside your Windows word processor you can insert Bible verses by means of the Windows feature called Dynamic Data Exchange (DDE). Like DVI, this method for inserting Bible verses into a word processor requires the word processor to be a Windows-based application. DOS-based applications do not support DDE. See **DDE** in this chapter.

DOS Word Processors and the Windows Clipboard

The Windows clipboard can be used to insert text into DOS-based non-Windows word processors and text editors. While this technique is not an

NEBRL feature, we are including this brief discussion for the sake of completeness.

> **NOTE:** This will work only if you are running Windows 95, or Windows 3.1 in Enhanced Mode.

To paste a Bible passage into a DOS word processor, do the following:

1. Copy text to the Windows clipboard.

2. Open the DOS-based program. Position the cursor where you want to insert text.

3. From the keyboard, press ALT+ENTER. The DOS window will reduce to less than full-screen size. Notice that the DOS window now has a Title Bar with the Control Menu button in the upper left corner. (The Title Bar and Control Menu are not visible when a DOS application is full-screen size.)

4. Click the Control Menu button, opening the Control Menu.

5. Click *Edit*. A small dialog box opens.

6. Click *Paste*. The text in the clipboard will be pasted into your document.

Copy Special and Copy

NEBRL provides two ways of copying text to the Windows clipboard for pasting into NEBRL notes or Windows word processors: Copy Special and Copy.

The Copy command allows you to copy selected text *fragments* (rather than only whole verses, articles, or notes) to the clipboard. The Copy command uses the standard Windows copy and paste commands from the **Edit** menu. Click and drag with the left mouse button over text in any of your books or notes to highlight and select it. Then select *Copy* from the **Edit** menu (ALT+E,C) [CTRL+C] (⌘+C). The text is now on the Windows clipboard, ready to be pasted into your notes or any document in a Windows word processor with the *Paste* command from the **Edit** menu.

Copy Special, on the other hand, copies complete Bible verses, non-Bible articles, search results, notes to the clipboard without the need for clicking and dragging over text to select it.

The Copy Special option allows you to copy data from NEBRL 2.1 to the Windows clipboard in four different formats:

- ASCII text.
- Unicode text.
- Rich Text Format (RTF) (which contains formatted text information).
- HTML text (HyperText Markup Language), the file format used to structure documents on the World Wide Web and to hyperlink them to other documents, sounds, videos, and images.

> **NOTE:** Rich Text Format (RTF) is a format which can be used to prepare data for use in a word processor that supports this format. Some word processors may not be able to take advantage of all RTF formatting.

Copied text can contain:

- A range of Bible verses from any Bible version in your library, complete with translator's notes, if desired.

- Text from any book in your library.

- Search results, with entire text of articles containing hits, if desired.

- Your notes, complete with note labels and referenced text, if desired.

Access the Copy Special dialog as follows:

- Select *Copy Special* from the **Edit** menu (ALT+E,I).

The Copy Special dialog opens (Fig. 6-10).

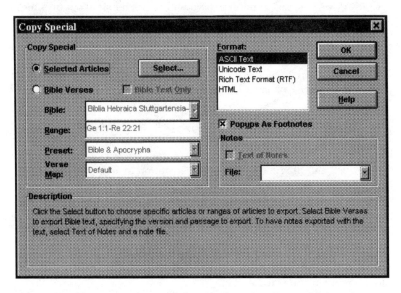

Figure 6-10 Copy Special Dialog: Copying Complete Text to Clipboard.

The Copy Special dialog takes on three different forms depending on what you are copying: Bible or non-Bible text, search results, or notes.

Copying Text

If the current active window is any window other than the Search Results window or a note window when you open the Copy Special dialog, it will provide options for copying Bible or non-Bible text (Fig. 6-10).

You may choose either of the following two options:

- **Selected Articles:** Copy selected articles from any of your books. Click *Select* to open the **Range Selection** dialog. Use the Available Items browser on the left to select books, chapters, articles to copy to the clipboard. Click the item you want to copy, then click and drag it over to the Selected Items list box, click *Add* to move it there, or right-click to open the right mouse menu and click *Add Item* (⌘+A). If you decide to remove an item from the Selected Items list box, click it, then click *Remove* (+R). Click *OK* when you are finished selecting items to copy.

- **Bible Verses:** Copy a range of Bible verses from a particular Bible version. From the drop-down list boxes select the Bible version and either a preset range of Bible books, or a special range of verses. If you do not select the Bible Text Only check box, Bible text plus any supplemental translator's notes will copy to the clipboard.

To copy any notes which are tied to the copied text:

- Click the Text of Notes box and select the appropriate note file from the drop-down list box. (The list box displays the names of note files which are currently open. If the note file you want is not listed, close the Copy Special dialog, open the note file, and then reopen the Copy Special dialog.)

Copying Search Results

If the Search Results window is the active window when you open the Copy Special dialog, it will provide options for copying your search results (Fig. 6-11).

You may choose one of the following three options:

- **Search Hit Descriptions:** Copy only the descriptions of the search hit locations (for Bibles, this would be the Bible reference, e.g., Gen. 1:1). The search hit descriptions are listed on the left side of the Search Results window.

- **Search Hits in Context:** Copy the search-hits-in-context line of text which appears on the right side of the Search Results window when you select Show Search Hits in Context.

- **Full Text of Search Hits:** Copy the complete article containing the search hit.

To copy any notes which are tied to the search hit references:

- Click the Text of Notes box and select the appropriate note file from the drop-down list box. (The list box displays the names of note files which are currently open. If the note file you want is not listed, close the Copy Special dialog, open the note file, and then reopen the Copy Special dialog.)

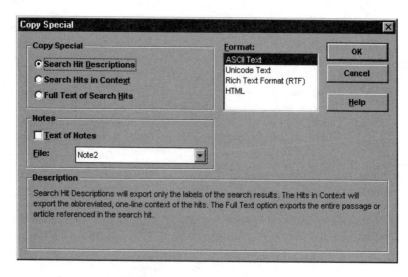

Figure 6-11 Copying Search Results to the Clipboard.

Copying Notes

If a note window is the active window when you open the Copy Special dialog, it will provide options for copying your notes (Fig. 6-12).

First, select the note file you want to copy to the clipboard from the dropdown list box. The note file you had open when you entered the Copy Spe-

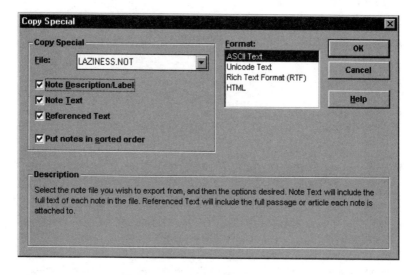

Figure 6-12 Copying Notes to the Clipboard.

cial dialog will display in the list box, however you may switch to a different note file if it is also open on the screen. If the note file you want is not listed, close the Copy Special dialog, open the note file, and then reopen the Copy Special dialog.

You may choose any or all of the following four options:

- **Note Description/Label:** Copy the note label (found on the left side of the Notes window), which indicates the location to which the note is tied.

- **Note Text:** Copy the text of the note.

- **Referenced Text:** Copy the book text to which the note is tied. This text is referenced by the note label. For example, if the note label is "Psalm 22:1," this option will copy the text of Psalm 22:1.

- **Put notes in sorted order:** If you select this option, the system will ignore your note arrangement and will copy the notes in the browser sorted order.

Dynamic Verse Insertion

NEBRL allows you to export Bible verses directly to your word processor document through the use of DVI. (To insert text other than Bible verses, use export or the clipboard.)

To export Bible verses into your word processor document with DVI do the following:

1. With your word processor as the active program on your screen, position your cursor at the location in your word processor document where you want the verses to be inserted. (The software need not necessarily be a word processor. Any Windows-based software which has an Edit-Paste function will work with DVI.)

2. Switch to NEBRL so it is the active program.

3. Click the DVI button in the upper left corner of your screen. The DVI dialog will open (Fig. 6-13).

(The DVI button can be relocated to any position on your screen by clicking in its title bar and, while holding down the left mouse button, dragging it to the desired location.)

4. In the Bibles list, click on the Bible version from which you want to extract verses.

5. In the Bible Reference box, enter the range of verses you wish to insert into your document. Click *Insert* to insert the verses at the cursor position in your document. Go to Edit Menu and choose *Paste*. Click *Cancel* to cancel the operation.

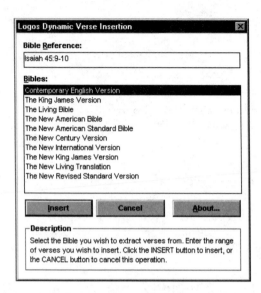

Figure 6-13 Dynamic Verse Insertion (DVI) Dialog.

The display of the DVI button on your screen can be toggled on and off. The button is displayed by default. (See **DDE/DVI** in chapter seven, "System Management.")

DVI and Windows 3.1x

If you receive an error while trying to insert a verse with DVI or DVI does not insert the selected verse into the selected document, check the FILES= setting in the file CONFIG.SYS. The value at the end of this line should be at least 20, preferably 30, for DVI to work properly in Windows 3.1x.

Dynamic Data Exchange

Windows has a feature called **Dynamic Data Exchange** (DDE) whereby different programs can exchange information. NEBRL allows you to import Bible verses directly into your word processor document through the use of DDE. (To insert text other than Bible verses, use export or the clipboard from within NEBRL.) A document template for Microsoft Word for Windows is supplied with NEBRL which allows you to do this.

For details on NEBRL DDE support for developing your own DDE macros, see Appendix C, **DDE Support**.

> **NOTE:** You *must* have the NEBRL directory (usually C:\LO-GOS20) in your Path statement in your AUTOEXEC.BAT file in order for the Word for Windows DDE macro to function. For in-

structions on how to edit the Path statement in this file, see your manual.

Microsoft Word for Windows Macro

To use the Microsoft Word for Windows macro, do the following:

1. Determine which version of Microsoft Word for Windows you have. (If you have version 6.0, skip to step 8 now.)

2. If you have version 2.1, copy the file LOGOS.DOT from your NEBRL directory (usually C:\LOGOS20) into your Word for Windows directory (usually C:\WINWORD). (You can do this from your Windows File Manager by clicking on the LOGOS.DOT file and then pressing F8 on your keyboard.) Now give it the destination directory, C:\WINWORD. Press ENTER.

3. Close File Manager. Run Word for Windows 2.0.

4. From the Word for Windows **File** menu select *New*.

5. Select the NEBRL document template from the Templates list. Click **OK**.

6. Whenever you want a reference or passage inserted into your Word for Windows document, select *Insert Verses* from the **Insert** menu.

7. The Insert Verses dialog box will open. You'll be prompted for a Bible verse or range of verses. Enter a passage and select the appropriate Bible version. Click **OK**.

8. If you have version 6.0 of Word for Windows, copy the file LOGOS.DOT from your NEBRL directory into your Word for Windows startup subdirectory (C:\WINWORD\STARTUP). Do this from Windows File Manager by clicking on the LOGOS.DOT file and then pressing F8 on your keyboard. Now give it the destination directory C:\WINWORD\STARTUP. Press ENTER.

The template will automatically install two toolbar buttons for the new macros.

Other DDE Applications

If you feel comfortable with writing DDE macros, you can add your own basic DDE support to other word processors and Windows applications that support DDE. See Appendix C, **DDE Support** for technical information.

Importing

The Import option allows you to import both note and topical index files from Logos 1.6, as well as note files from Parsons QuickVerse, Holy Scriptures, and WordSearch.

To import note files:

1. Select *Import* from the **File** menu (ALT+F,I).

2. The **Open** dialog appears (Fig. 6-14). From the List Files of Type drop-down list box select the type of file you want to import into a NEBRL note file.

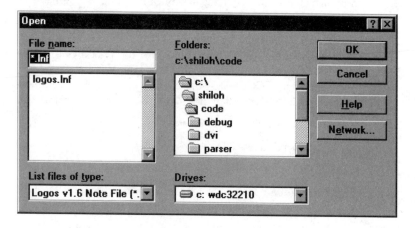

Figure 6-14 Import Open Dialog.

3. From the File Name list box, select the file you want to import. Click *OK* to import the file. A new note file is created. When you save this file, you will assign it a name with a .NOT extension.

Importing from Parsons QuickVerse

Before you import notes from Parsons QuickVerse, you must *export* the file from QuickVerse. NEBRL does not import QuickVerse notes in their native QuickVerse format.

Importing from Holy Scriptures

Before you import notes from Holy Scriptures, you must *export* the file from Holy Scriptures. There are three things to be observed:

- Select *Export to File*.

- Choose to include: Text, Notes, and Verse numbers.

- Export entire books (can be a range of books, but entire books must be used).

7

System Management

NEBRL provides system management functions for fine-tuning your system. Managing your NEBRL library falls into five primary areas: setting your preferences; unlocking titles; moving/copying titles; rebuilding the Global Word Index, and backing up and restoring your system settings.

Preferences

Customize certain NEBRL features according to your personal preferences by utilizing the **Preferences** dialog (Fig. 7-1). If you click *OK* in this dialog

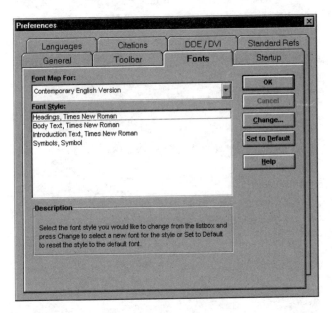

Figure 7-1 Preferences Dialog: Fonts Tab Panel.

after making changes, the changes will be permanently saved. If you click *Cancel*, any changes you have made will be ignored.

To access the Preferences dialog, do the following:

■ Select *Preferences* from the **Edit** menu (ALT+E,F).

The available options in the Preferences dialog are accessed by clicking on the various tab panels. These options are as follows:

Fonts

Click this tab panel to customize fonts for a particular book (Fig. 7-1). To change fonts, do the following:

1. In the Font Map For box select the book for which you want to change fonts. Display the book list by clicking the down arrow on the right end of the box. Scroll down the list and click the desired book.

2. In the Font Style list box select the font style you wish to change (Body Text, Headings, Greek Body Text, etc.). Click *Change*. The **Font** dialog will appear.

3. Select the new font. Click *OK*.

Citations

Click the Citations tab panel to customize the format NEBRL uses for appending bibliographic citations when copying, printing, or exporting text from your books (Fig. 7-2).

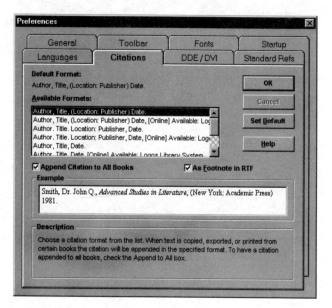

Figure 7-2 Preferences Dialog: Citations Tab Panel.

To customize citations, do the following:

1. Click the desired citation format in the Available Formats list box.

2. To have a citation appended to all text, click the Append Citation to All Books check box. If this option is not selected, citations will only be appended from certain books at the publishers' discretion.

3. To have citations formatted as footnotes in RTF (Rich Text Format) for use in standard word processors, click the As Footnote in RTF check box. The text will include a footnote reference and the citation will automatically become a footnote.

4. Click *Set Default* to set your choice for the new default citation format.

General

Click the General tab panel to customize general NEBRL features (Fig. 7-3).

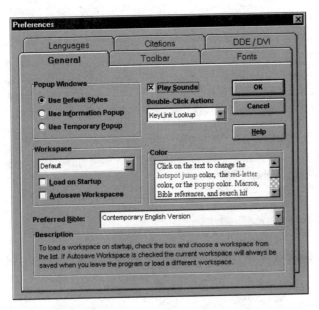

Figure 7-3 Preferences Dialog: General Tab Panel.

Popup Windows

NEBRL uses two different styles of popup windows: Temporary Popups and Information Popups. Some types of information pop onto the screen in temporary popup windows which will disappear when you click anywhere else on the screen. Other types of information pop onto the screen in information popup windows which remain on the screen until you close them by clicking on the close button in the window's upper left corner. Click the appropriate box to allow NEBRL to control the styles of popups used, or force all popups to be one kind or the other.

Preferred Bible

Select your Preferred Bible from the list box. NEBRL will open this Bible if you click a Bible reference in another book and there is no other Bible yet open on the screen. In addition, this Bible will be opened first if you click the New Bible Window button on the Toolbar and it is not already open.

Play Sounds

Check this box if you want NEBRL to play sounds. NEBRL installs preset sounds for various sound events. The installation will set these sound events by default to supplied .WAV files. If you wish, you may relink these sound events to your own specific sound files.

To relink sound events:

1. Switch to the Windows Control Panel and choose the **Sound** dialog.

2. Make sure the Enable System Sounds box is checked and that you have a properly installed sound card and speakers.

3. Assuming you have sounds working properly, scroll through the Events list to find the NEBRL events. These events relate to such things as the startup and exit of the program, searching, popups, etc. Link each one of these events with one of the .WAV files in the File list.

4. After you have linked all of the sound events with individual sounds, close the Sound dialog by clicking *OK* and then close the Control Panel dialog by double-clicking the Close button in the upper left corner of the dialog. Return to NEBRL.

Double-Click Action

From the pull-down list select the action you want performed when you double-click on a word in a book. The choices are Nothing, KeyLink Lookup, Topic Search, Topic Search All Titles, Speed Search, and Speed Search All Titles. Set this option to the type of search you most often perform. The less-used choices can then easily be accessed from the right mouse menu. (For right mouse menu searching, see **Right Mouse Searching** in chapter four, "Searching.")

Color

To change the color of special text within NEBRL, click the hot spot item whose color you want to change (popups, macros, search hits, etc.). The **Color** dialog will open. Click the desired color or define a new color. Click *OK* to store the color and return to the General tab panel.

Toolbar

Click the Toolbar tab panel to customize your Toolbar behavior (Fig. 7-4).

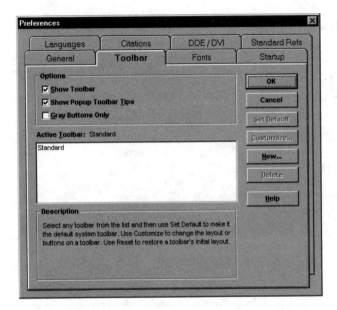

Figure 7-4 Preferences Dialog: Toolbar Tab Panel.

If you use the Toolbar, check the Show Toolbar box so the Toolbar will be displayed.

If you like to see the Toolbar Tips which pop up when you position your cursor on a Toolbar button, check the Show Popup Toolbar Tips box.

For monochrome monitors check the Gray Buttons Only box.

Select any Toolbar from the list and click *Set Default* to make it the default system Toolbar.

Customize

To change the layout of the buttons on a Toolbar, click *Customize*. The **Customize Toolbar** dialog will open (Fig. 7-5). This dialog consists of two lists. The list on the left contains the available actions which are not being used on the Toolbar. The list on the right contains the current state of the Toolbar. Scrolling down the list displays the current Toolbar from left to right.

To customize the Toolbar:

1. Select actions from the list on the left by clicking them, and click the *Add* button to move them to the Toolbar on the right. The *Remove* button removes selected commands from the Toolbar and returns them to the list on the left.

2. After adding a button to the Toolbar on the right, click the *Move Up* button to move the button on the Toolbar. As the button moves, you will

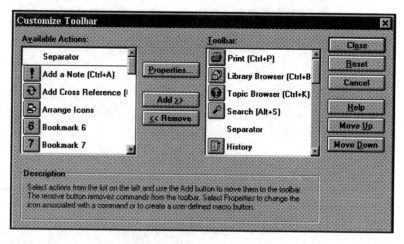

Figure 7-5 Preferences Dialog: Customize Toolbar.

see it moving from right to left on the Toolbar in the NEBRL main window. If you want to undo your moves, click *Reset*. Add Separators onto the Toolbar to put space between the buttons as desired.

3. When you have finished customizing the Toolbar, click *Close*. If you decide to undo all of your changes, click *Cancel*.

Change Icons

Click *Properties* to change the icon associated with a command or to create a user-defined macro button. The **Properties** dialog opens (Fig. 7-6).

To associate a new icon with a given action:

1. Click the desired action in the Action list, highlighting it.

2. Scroll across the group of icons on the right to locate the one you want to associate with the selected action. Click the icon to link it to the action.

Macros

Macros are primarily for advanced users. The NEBRL macro commands are included for those who wish to create their own unique functions within NEBRL. We have included a few sample macros to demonstrate what is possible.

To create a new macro which you can then associate with an icon:

1. Click *Add Macro*, opening the **Add User Macro** dialog (Fig. 7-7).

2. Enter a name for the new macro, and then type the text of the macro in the Macro Text field. Macros should be entered without unnecessary spaces and with balanced parentheses.

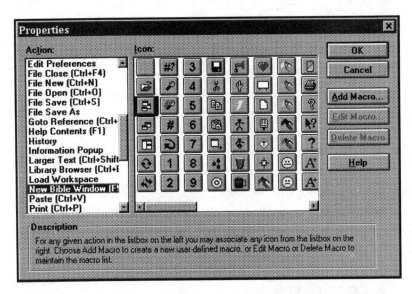

Figure 7-6 Preferences Dialog: Change Icons Associated with a Command.

Use the *Edit Macro* and *Delete Macro* buttons to maintain the macro list.

Following is a list of macro commands and their argument fields:

- LoadWorkspace("S"); Load the workspace named S.

- SaveWorkspaceAs("S"); Save the workspace named S.

- SaveWorkspace(); Save the workspace under its current name, which may be default.

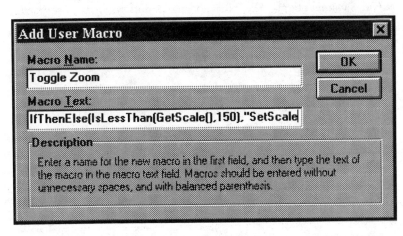

Figure 7-7 Preferences Dialog: Add User Macros.

- OpenBook("S"); Open the book with the name S (e.g., KJV or NEW NAVES).

- DDEExecute("S","S","S","S"); Execute a program with S=application path; S=Server name; S=Topic name; S=Data.

- GoToToday(i); Goes to day i (1–365) in a book organized by days (e.g., Morning and Evening).

- GoToBookmark(i); Go to Bookmark i (1–9).

- GoToURL("S"); Go to Universal Resource Location S. Used to go to Internet locations.

- History(); Open the History dialog.

- Back(); Go back to previous location. Backtrack bookmark.

- SetScale(u); Set the scale of the screen display (font size) to u (unsigned integer = percentage, e.g., 25 = 25%, 100 = 100%, 150 = 150%).

- GetScale(i); Returns i, the percentage of the current screen display scaling (e.g., 150 = 150%).

- PlaySound("S"); Play the .wav file named S (e.g., chimes.wav).

- Exit(); Exit the program.

- About(); Display the About dialog.

- ShowWordList(); Display the Global Word List.

- HideWordList(); Hide the Global Word List.

- ShowFloatingPopup(); Display the floating popup window (Information Popups).

- HideFloatingPopup(); Hide the floating popup window (Information Popups).

- ShowBrowser(); Display the Library Browser.

- HideBrowser(); Hide the Library Browser.

- SetCurRef("S"); Go to Bible reference S (e.g., Exodus 12:37).

- TopicSearch("S"); Execute a Topic Search for topic S. Function returns an integer, 0 if no match, 1 if there is at least one match.

- SpeedSearch("S"); Execute a Speed Search on word S. Function returns an integer, 0 if no match, 1 if there is at least one match.

- ReferenceSearch("S"); Execute a Reference Search on Bible reference S. Function returns an integer, 0 if no match, 1 if there is at least one match.

- ExecProgram("S",u); Start program S with a state of u (Minimized, maximized, etc.).

- IfThen(i,"S"); If i is true, then execute S, where i is any command that returns an integer (e.g., SpeedSearch), and S is any command.

- IfThenElse(i,"S","S"); If i is true, then execute S (#1), else execute S (#2). Same as above.

- Not(i); Turns i into not i.

- DeleteMark("S"); Delete Mark (flag) S.

- IsMark("S"); Returns value of Mark (flag) S.

- SaveMark("S"); Saves current value in Mark (flag) S. S can be any name you assign, and you may create as many different marks as desired, giving each one a unique name. Then test each mark as desired to see if it exists or has been deleted.

- Repeat(u,"S"); Repeat command S, u (unsigned integer) number of times.

- SetWindowPos(u,i,i,i,i,u); Set window size and position according to standard Windows parameters.

- ShowWindow(i); Display Window i.

- Activate(); Activate (restore) minimized program.

- Minimize(); Minimize the current window.

- Maximize(); Maximize the current window.

- CopySelection(); Copy current selected text to the Windows clipboard.

- SetRedLetterColor(i,i,i); Set red letter color to the RGB values of i, i, and i.

- Multiply(i,i); Multiply i times i. Returns the value i.

- Divide(i,i); Divide i (#1) by i (#2). Returns the value i.

- Add(i,i); Add i plus i. Returns the value i.

- Subtract(i,i); Subtract i (#2) from i (#1). Returns the value i.

- IsEqualTo(i,i); If i is equal to i, return i=1, otherwise i=0.

- IsGreaterThan(i,i); If i (#1) is greater than i (#2), return i=1, otherwise i=0.

- IsLessThan(i,i); If i (#1) is less than i (#2), return i=1, otherwise i=0.

- SetResourceDLL("S"); Change the application's base language by changing to the .DLL named S. For example, if you change the application's base language to Spanish, all of the menus will display in Spanish.

This sample macro starts the Windows Calculator.

```
ExecProgram("CALC.EXE",0)
```

This sample macro toggles the screen text between 100% and 150% zoom.

```
IfThenElse(IsLessThan(GetScale(),150),"SetScale
(150)","SetScale(100)")
```

This sample macro copies highlighted text to the clipboard and then automatically pastes it into Word for Windows.

```
CopySelection();
DDEExecute("c:\winword6\winword.exe","winword",
"System","Paste")
```

Word Processor Macros

WordPerfect

The macro for WordPerfect is designed to work with WordPerfect for Windows versions 6.0 and newer. This macro does not work well with any earlier version of WordPerfect for Windows.

Languages

Click the Languages tab panel to customize the way your system deals with various languages (Fig. 7-8).

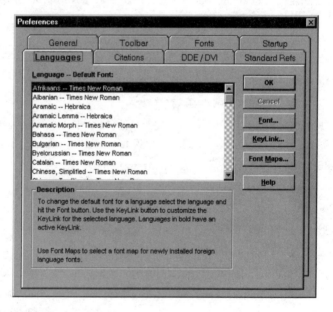

Figure 7-8 Preferences Dialog: Languages Tab Panel.

Default Font

To change the default font for a language:

1. Click the desired language in the list box, highlighting it.
2. Click *Font* to open the **Font** dialog. Select the font you want to use to display the language. Click *OK* to close the Font dialog and return to the Languages tab panel.

KeyLink

KeyLinks are links between a particular language and the default type of search NEBRL will perform when you select a word in that language. For example, if you select a Greek word in a book, the KeyLink will determine the default lexicon you want NEBRL to search and whether you want to perform a Topic search or a full text search.

The *KeyLink* button allows you to define the KeyLink for a selected language. Clicking *KeyLink* opens the **Define KeyLink** dialog (Fig. 7-9).

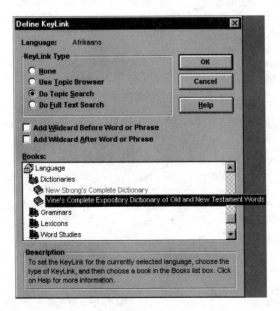

Figure 7-9 Preferences Dialog: Define KeyLinks.

> **NOTE:** You can access the Define KeyLink dialog without entering the Preferences dialog. Inside any document window, click the right mouse button, opening the right mouse menu. Click *Define KeyLink* (⌘+D). The Define KeyLink dialog will open.

To set the KeyLink for the language:

1. Before you open the Define KeyLink Dialog, in the Languages tab panel click the language for which you want to define the KeyLink.

2. Go to the Define KeyLink dialog. Click the type of KeyLink desired:

   ■ *Use Topic Browser.* With this option selected, when you select a word in this language, NEBRL will open the Topic Browser to the selected word if the word is specified as a topic in the KeyLink book. If the selected word is not defined as a topic, NEBRL will ask if you want to open the Topic Browser anyway so you can check other topics.

- *Do Topic Search.* NEBRL will perform a Topic search of the KeyLink book. If matches are found, they will be listed in a search results window. If the selected word is not defined as a topic, NEBRL will ask if you want to open the main Search dialog to perform a different search.

  NOTE: Both of the preceding KeyLink types provide essentially the same results when successful, i.e., a list of articles in the specified book related to the topic being searched. The difference between the two KeyLink types relates primarily to what happens when they do *not* find a match. The *Topic Browser* type offers to open the Topic Browser anyway, allowing you to scroll through the book's list of topics in search of other articles that might be relevant even though they are not an exact match. The *Topic Search* type offers to open the main Search dialog, allowing you to construct a search of any book(s) in your library in an attempt to find information relevant to your original request.

- *Do Full Text Search.* NEBRL will perform a full concordance search for any occurrence of the word in the KeyLink book. This type of search will generally find more matches, however some of the matches may not be as relevant as those located in the other two types of searches, since this search is not restricted to locating articles with the word in question as a *topic* of the articles.

3. When selecting either Topic Search or Full Text Search, you have the option available of checking a box to add a wildcard either before or after the word (phrase) for which you will be searching. For example, when you perform a KeyLink search by clicking on "faith," if you would like the search to include "faithful" and "faithfulness" as well, click the Add Wildcard After Word or Phrase box.

4. Select the KeyLink book. As you scroll down the book list, open the appropriate book categories by clicking their icons or double-clicking their titles to find the appropriate book to KeyLink to the language. The books which contain the language will appear highlighted on the list, the inappropriate books will be greyed.

5. Click *Font Maps* to select a font map for a newly-installed foreign language font. When you install a new foreign language font other than the fonts supplied by NEBRL, you must inform NEBRL of the correct font map for the font so that NEBRL will properly interpret the characters on the font.

DDE/DVI

Click the DDE/DVI tab panel to set up the way NEBRL will interact with Parsons QuickVerse Bible software and both NEBRL and Parsons atlas programs by means of Dynamic Data Exchange (DDE), as well as applications with Edit-Paste functions (typically word processors) by means of Dynamic Verse Insertion (DVI) (Fig. 7-10).

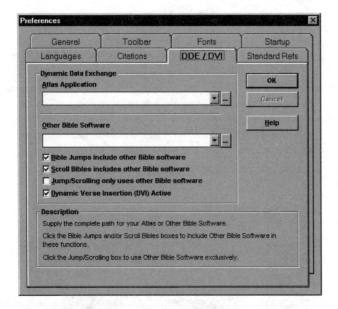

Figure 7-10 Preferences Dialog: DDE/DVI Tab Panel.

In the edit controls supply the complete path to each application.

For Logos Bible Atlas you would type:

```
C:\LBA\LBA.EXE
```

For Parsons Bible Atlas you would type:

```
C:\PCBAWIN\PCBAWIN.EXE
```

These examples assume you have installed the software in the default directory. If you installed your atlas to a different path, use that path instead.

Click the Bible Jumps and/or Scroll Bibles boxes to include other Bible software in these functions.

Click the Jump/Scrolling box to use other Bible software exclusively.

Unclick the Dynamic Verse Insertion Active box to turn off DVI if you do not plan to insert Bible verses from NEBRL into your Windows word processor. DVI can be turned back on (the DVI button will reappear in the upper left corner of your screen) by clicking this box again.

For more information on linking DDE to other software, see the instructions in the *Readme* file. Double click on the Nelson Read Me icon in the *Nelson Electronic Library* program group.

Standardized References

Some books have **SR Hotspots**, which are jumps to a particular **Standardized Reference**. In order for the *Nelson Electronic Bible Reference Library* to know which book to use, you must configure this SR Scheme to use a particular book. If the SR Scheme isn't configured to use a particular book, it will use the first book in the library it finds that supports this SR Scheme. If the SR Scheme is configured to use a particular book, it will use that book unless it is not currently in the library. If this is the case, it will use the first book in the library it finds that supports this SR Scheme.

Click on the Standard Refs tab to customize the available SR schemes (Fig. 7-11).

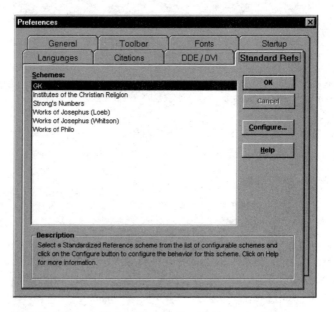

Figure 7-11 Preferences Dialog: Standardized References Panel.

Schemes

The names of all available schemes will be listed in this list box. Select the scheme whose behavior you want to configure and click *Configure*. This will open the **Define SR Scheme Behavior dialog** (Fig. 7-11a).

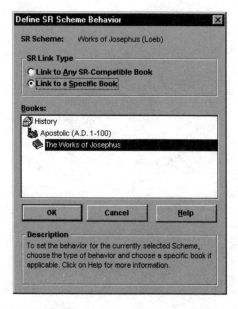

Figure 7-11a Define SR Scheme Behavior Dialog (from Standardized Ref Panel).

Define SR Scheme Behavior

This dialog allows the user to define the behavior for a particular **Standardized Reference scheme**.

Scheme Behavior

To define the behavior for the scheme, click on the radio button which specifies the desired behavior. The choices are:

- *Link to any SR-Compatible Book*. This option causes **hotspots** to use the first book it finds in your library that supports this SR scheme.

- *Link to a Specific Book*. This option causes hotspots to use only the book selected in the Books list.

Books

Use this list to select the specific book to which hotspots using this SR scheme should jump.

Startup

Click the Startup tab panel to configure NEBRL startup behavior. Upon startup, NEBRL can either do nothing, load books, load a workspace, or run a macro (Fig. 7-12).

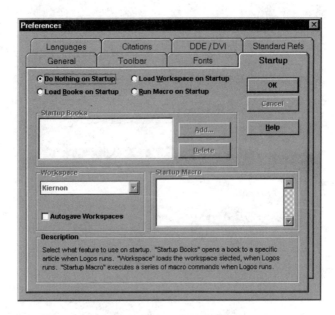

Figure 7-12 Preferences Dialog: Startup Tab Panel.

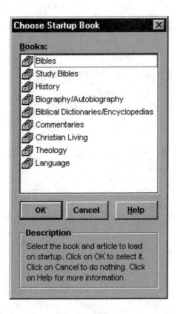

Figure 7-12a Choose Startup Book Dialog

Do Nothing

Click on this radio button to do nothing on startup. All of the other settings in the panel will be ignored if this is selected.

Load Books

Click on this radio button to load the books in the *Start Books* listbox. To add one or more books, click on the *Add* button. This will open the **Choose Startup Book** dialog (Fig. 7-12a). Click on *Delete* to delete the selected article or book in the *Startup Books* listbox.

Load Workspace

Click on this radio button to load a workspace on startup. Use the drop-down listbox in the Workspace section of this panel to select which workspace to load on startup. Turn on *Autosave Workspace* to save the workspace upon exiting NEBRL. If *Autosave Workspace* is turned off, the workspace will only be saved when you select *Save Workspace* from the **File** menu (alt+f,v).

To load a workspace while you are in NEBRL, select *Load Workspace* from the **File** menu (alt+f,w). The **Load Workspace** dialog appears. Select the desired workspace from the list and click *OK*.

To have NEBRL save the current status of your workspace *automatically* every time you quit the program or load a different workspace, check the Autosave Workspace box.

Run Macro

Click on the radio button to run the **macros** listed in the Startup Macro control upon startup.

Unlocking Titles

NEBRL enables you to conveniently purchase titles as you need them. Rather than having to buy a large quantity of books all at one time, you can invest in individual books by merely placing a phone call to Thomas Nelson. NEBRL unlocks the book which already resides on your CD-ROM library disk, and you may begin using it immediately.

Browsing Locked Books and Collections of Books

You can browse through and unlock locked books and collections of books using the **Locked Book and Collection Browser** (Fig. 7-13).

Access the Locked Book and Collection Browser as follows:

■ Select *Unlock Books or Collections* from the **Tools** menu (ALT+T,U).

The descriptions and prices of individual books, and collections of books, can be viewed in the **Description** field on the right. The dialog will only enable options that are available for the book or collection and distributor you have selected.

To view a title description:

1. Select the distributor you wish to purchase the item from using the **Distributor** drop-down listbox. A complete list of distributors whose Logos or Thomas Nelson products you've installed will be contained in this drop-down listbox. (All U.S. customers call the Nelson toll-free number.)

2. Select either the **Books** or **Collections** radio button in the **View** section of the dialog to see a list of books or collections of books you can unlock.

3. Click on the title of the desired item in the list box on the left.

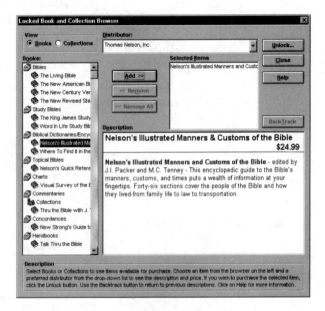

Figure 7-13 Locked Book and Collection Browser.

4. The description and price will display in the **Description** area to the right.

To add to the list of books or collections to be unlocked:

1. Select the desired book or collection in the *Books* or *Collections* list.

2. Click on the Add button.

3. Keep adding items until you have added all of the items you would like to unlock.

4. To remove one or all of the selected items, use the *Remove* or the *Remove All* button.

To unlock the selected items, you may do so in one of two ways:

■ By contacting the distributor over the phone. Click *Unlock* to begin the process of unlocking the items over the phone. You will need to call the distributor and purchase the items. See the **Unlock a Book or Collection dialog** for more information.

■ For distributors that support it, by contacting the distributor over the World Wide Web. Click *Web Unlock* to begin the process of unlocking the items over the World Wide Web (Internet). You will need to contact the distributor and purchase the item using their Web Site. See the **Unlock a Book or Collection via the Web dialog** for more information.

After this is done, you may select additional items for unlocking. After you are finished viewing descriptions and unlocking items, close the **Locked Book and Collections Browser** by clicking *Close*. If you have unlocked any items, NEBRL will prompt you to backup your system files and then to restart NEBRL so that your newly unlocked books will be available for use.

Unlocking Books and Collections of Books

The **Unlock** dialog (Fig. 7-13a) appears when you click *Unlock* in the **Locked Book and Collection Browser**. This dialog allows you to purchase and unlock the item you have selected in the **Locked Book and Collection Browser**.

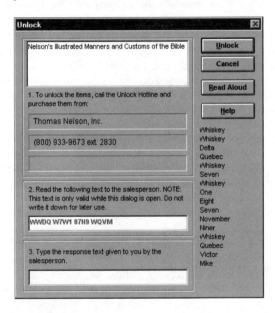

Figure 7-13a Unlock Dialog.

1. Call the Unlock Hotline number provided in the Unlock Book or Collection dialog.

2. Purchase the item or items from the representative.

3. Do either of the following:

   ■ If your computer has sound: When the Thomas Nelson representative requests the unlock code, hold the mouthpiece of your phone next to your computer's speaker and click the Read Aloud button. NEBRL will read the unlock code to the representative.

   ■ Read the unlock code to the representative. The unlock code will be spelled out on the right using words for the letters (Alpha, Bravo, etc).

NOTE: The unlock code is only valid while the Unlock dialog is open. Do not write it down for later use as it will be unusable after the dialog is closed.

4. In the lower box, type the response code given to you by the representative.

5. Click Unlock.

Title Librarian

Move books from the CD-ROM to your hard drive or move them back to the CD-ROM when you have finished using them or if you merely need more disk space. Book access and searching are faster when the book resides on your hard disk drive. However, books use a great deal of disk space and it may not always be convenient to have many of them located on your hard disk. It is probably advisable to keep only your most-used books on your hard disk.

Title Librarian makes it easy to move or copy your books from drive to drive or from directory to directory on the same drive. *Do not* move your book files using standard DOS commands or File Manager. You must use Title Librarian if you want NEBRL to be able to locate your books. You copy and move books from the **Title Librarian Move/Copy** dialog (Fig. 7-14).

Figure 7-14 Title Librarian Dialog.

To access the Title Librarian dialog, do the following:

■ Select *Title Librarian* from the **Tools** menu (ALT+T,L).

Move a book as follows:

1. Select a book by clicking it in the list, highlighting it.

2. Check or uncheck the Books and Indices boxes as appropriate to move both the book text file and/or the book's index file. As you check and uncheck these two boxes the data box below the book list will display the total bytes of selected data that will be moved (Fig. 7-14).

3. Click *Move* to move the book. Normally you would use *Move* when moving a book from the CD-ROM to the hard disk or back again, because you want NEBRL to use the book from its new location. Copy is appropriate only when making a copy of a book to another directory on your hard disk. After copying a book NEBRL will continue to use the book from its original location.

   ■ Do *not* use *Remove* unless you never want to use a book again. This button only exists to remove a book from the Library Browser. However, you can restore all removed books to your library by eliminating and rebuilding the map file.

Rebuilding the Global Word Index

The Global Word Index provides a list of all words used in all of your books. It is helpful when you are searching for a word and you want to know all of the forms and spellings used for that word in your library. For example, if you are searching for the word "color," it would be helpful to know that it is spelled both "color" and "colour" in your library. This knowledge will assist you in locating all occurrences of the word.

When you add books to or remove books from your library, you must rebuild the Global Word Index if you want the list of words to be complete. It is *not* necessary to rebuild the list for the NEBRL search engine to work properly. This list exists only for your convenience so you can determine exactly what words exist in your library.

Rebuilding the Global Word Index can be time consuming. The time it takes will depend on the size of your library. Plan accordingly before you ask NEBRL to rebuild the Global Word Index.

To rebuild the Global Word Index, do one of the following:

■ When you start NEBRL, if the system determines that the current state of the Global Word Index does not match the books in your library, you will be asked if you want to rebuild the index. If you have time, click *OK*. Otherwise, click *No*, and rebuild it at a more convenient time.

■ Select *Rebuild Global Word Index* from the **Tools** menu (ALT+T,R). You will be warned that this process might take a while, and you will be prompted to confirm your choice. If you want to rebuild the index, click *Yes*, otherwise click *No*.

Backup and Restore System Settings

System settings include such things as the map file which tells NEBRL where to find your books. Some books may be on your hard disk drive, some may be on a CD-ROM. Also, NEBRL knows which books you have unlocked. If you were to run setup again to reinstall NEBRL, these system settings would be lost unless you have backed up (saved) this information so that after reinstalling the software, you can restore your system to its original condition.

Backing up system settings uses the **Backup System Files** dialog (Fig. 7-15).

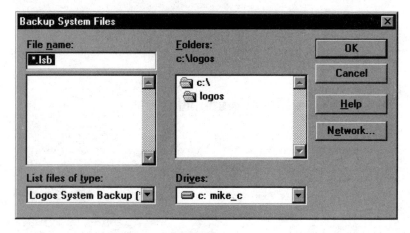

Figure 7-15 Backup System Files Dialog.

To backup your system settings:

1. Select *Backup NEBRL System Files* from the **Tools** menu (ALT+T,B). The **Backup System Files** dialog opens.

2. Change to the directory where you want the backup stored or accept the default. NEBRL supplies the file name for you, "logos.lsb." Click *OK* to make the backup.

Restoring system settings uses the **Restore From Backup** dialog.

To restore your system settings:

1. Select *Restore System Files from Backup* from the **Tools** menu (ALT+T,E). The **Restore From Backup** dialog opens.

2. NEBRL will have located your most recent backup of system files and supplied the appropriate file name and directory for you. Click *OK* to restore your system.

Rebuild Filemap

The map file tells NEBRL where your books are located. Should your map file become damaged or be deleted, you can rebuild it with the Rebuild Filemap dialog (Fig. 7-16).

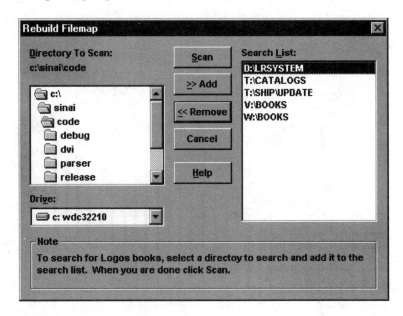

Figure 7-16 Rebuild Filemap Dialog.

To access the Rebuild Filemap dialog:

1. Select *Rebuild Filemap* from the **Tools** menu (ALT+T,F).

2. Select the directories where books are located, and then click *Scan*.

   NOTE: NEBRL will search the directories recursively. For example, if you have books located in various directories on your C hard drive, you could just enter c: as the directory to be scanned. NEBRL will then search all of this drive's subdirectories.

3. NEBRL will locate the directories which contain books and rebuild the map file accordingly.

4. The Scan Results dialog displays the number of directories which contain NEBRL books and the number of books found (both locked and un-

locked). If, after viewing the results in this dialog you realize that you have books in directories that you forgot to scan, you may select *Scan Again*. Otherwise, click *OK*. The logos.map file has been rebuilt so that when you next open NEBRL, it will search all directories which contain NEBRL books. All unlocked books will be available immediately. All locked books will be available for unlocking as desired.

Logos System Error

The map file tells NEBRL where your books are located. Should your map file become damaged or be deleted, NEBRL may not be able to find any books to load when it is started (Fig. 7-16a).

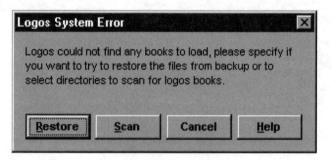

Figure 7-16a Logos System Error Dialog.

To tell NEBRL how to load your books do one of the following:

■ Click *Restore* to use the **Restore System Settings Dialog** to restore system settings previously saved using the **Backup System Settings Dialog**.

■ Click *Scan* to use the **Rebuild Filemap Dialog** to scan your system for books to load.

■ Click *Cancel* to close NEBRL without loading any books or making any changes to your NEBRL system settings.

8
Greek and Hebrew Study Tools

For those who are fluent in Greek and/or Hebrew, this chapter will discuss how to use the Greek and Hebrew language tools available in NEBRL. This chapter can also be useful for those who know little or no Greek and Hebrew. The system's ability to access Greek and Hebrew study tools even from an English translation expands the range of study tools available to those unfamiliar with the original biblical languages. In this chapter you will learn how to:

- View the Greek and Hebrew text, alone or with accompanying translation.

- Find the Greek or Hebrew word from which any English word was translated.

- Obtain grammatical information, such as part of speech, lemma, and brief definitions, for particular Greek and Hebrew words.

- View and use the Greek and Hebrew lexicons.

- Search the Greek and Hebrew texts in a variety of ways.

- Intermix multiple languages (including Greek and Hebrew) into one search request.

- Perform morphological searches.

Viewing Greek and Hebrew Texts

If you have Greek and/or Hebrew texts in your NEBRL electronic library, you can display them just as you would any other book. The Hebrew text is generally the Old Testament, while the Greek text can be one of several different versions of the New Testament text. Also available is the Septuagint, a Greek translation of the Old Testament from the original Hebrew.

Treat these texts as you would English texts. You can search them as well as copy text from them into your notes or a word processor. When searching Greek and Hebrew texts, you need not concern yourself with accents, breathing marks, special forms such as final sigmas. These are ignored by the search engine.

It's Greek to Me!

The system is designed to enable those who are not familiar with Greek and Hebrew to utilize the various Greek and Hebrew texts, as well as lexicons and dictionaries.

Example: In Genesis 1:1 (KJV) you see the English word, "created." You do not know Hebrew, but you would like to know what Hebrew word is translated "created" in this verse and you would like to see more lexical information about this Hebrew word. For example, you would like to see additional definitions as well as where else and how else it is used in the Old Testament.

There is one method for moving from English to Hebrew and an additional method for moving from English to Greek to solve these types of problems. One method uses the King James Version and Strong's numbers for both Greek and Hebrew. The other method (for Greek only) utilizes the New American Standard Bible and the Nestle-Aland Greek New Testament.

King James Version and Strong's Numbers

About 100 years ago, Dr. Strong keyed the English text of the King James Version of the Bible to the Hebrew and Greek words behind the translation, using numbers. The resulting numerical index from the King James English to the Greek and Hebrew is called *Strong's Concordance*, and the numbers which are used are called Strong's numbers.

NEBRL allows the user to access Strong's numbers while using the King James text. Strong's numbers can be accessed only when using the KJV because it is the individual words of the KJV to which the numbers are keyed.

A Strong's number leads to a definition in *Strong's Enhanced Lexicon* for the Greek or Hebrew word behind the number. This definition includes the Greek or Hebrew lemma (dictionary-form of word, lexeme) behind the word. This lemma leads to definitions and word studies in Greek and Hebrew lexicons and dictionaries.

The solution to studying a Hebrew word without knowing Hebrew, using Strong's numbers, is as follows:

1. **Select the English word you want to study in Hebrew.** Open the KJV to Genesis 1:1. Position the mouse cursor over the word "created."

2. **Find the word's Strong's number.** There are three ways to locate the Strong's number:

   ■ When you position the mouse cursor over a word in the KJV, the Strong's number keyed to the word will display in the Status Bar at the bottom of the screen.

■ When you position the mouse cursor over a word in the KJV, the cursor has an asterisk (*) beside it. This indicates that there is hidden information associated with the word. To display this information, click the *right* mouse button on the word "created," opening the right mouse menu. Click **Information**. A floating popup window opens, displaying the Strong's number, "1254" (Fig. 8-1).

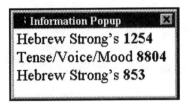

Figure 8-1 Information Popup.

■ Strong's numbers and TVM numbers can be viewed inline in the KJV text if desired. To display Strong's and TVM numbers inline in the KJV, select *Inline Strong's/TVM* from the **View** menu (ALT+V,V). Both Strong's and TVM numbers will display inline (Fig. 8-2). To turn off the display of these numbers, select the option again from the **Edit** menu.

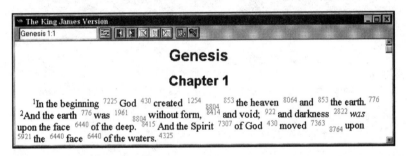

Figure 8-2 Inline Strong's and TVM Numbers.

3. **Use the Strong's number to locate related articles on the word in** *Strong's Enhanced Lexicon*. Locate articles using any of the following methods:

■ If you found the Strong's number merely by looking at the Status Bar, you must manually type the number into the Search Query box in the main Search dialog. Change the Search Type to Topic. Change the Language to Hebrew Strong's Numbers. Change the Search Range to *Strong's Enhanced Lexicon*. Click **Search**. NEBRL will locate the article on Strong's number 1254.

■ With the Information popup open, click the *right* mouse button on 1254, opening the right mouse menu. Click *KeyLink* (⌘+L). If you have properly set up KeyLink for Strong's numbers, the system should perform a Topic search, a Speed search, or open the Topic Browser on *Strong's Enhanced Lexicon* (depending on how you defined the Strong's number KeyLink), locating appropriate articles. (For details on defining KeyLinks, see **Languages** in chapter seven, "System Management.")

- With the Information popup open, click the *right* mouse button on 1254, opening the right mouse menu. Click any of the Topic search or Speed search options, depending on your interests.

- If you displayed the Strong's number inline (Fig. 8-2), left click on an inline Strong's number to bring up the lexicon's article on that number.

4. **Locate the word's lemma in the Strong's article.** Using any of the above methods, locate and open the Strong's Lexicon article on number 1254 (Fig. 8-3). Notice in the article the line which reads: "GK - 1343 et al." The Hebrew word which follows is the lemma for the Hebrew word translated "created" in Genesis 1:1. You can find this word without knowing anything about Hebrew!

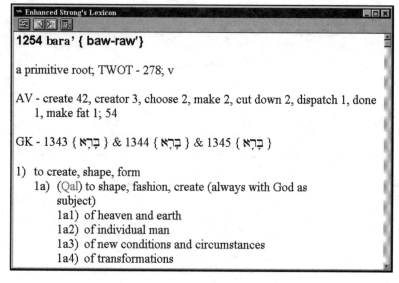

Figure 8-3 Strong's Lexicon Article: Number 1254.

5. **Use the lemma to locate appropriate articles on the word in Greek or Hebrew lexicons, dictionaries, etc.** Click the right mouse button on FRF.B, opening the right mouse menu. Click *KeyLink* (⌨+L). If you have properly set up KeyLink for Hebrew, the system should perform a Topic search, a Speed search, or open the Topic Browser on your favorite Hebrew lexicon (depending on how you defined the Hebrew KeyLink), locating appropriate articles. (For details on defining KeyLinks, see **Languages** in chapter seven, "System Management.")

New American Standard Bible and Nestle-Aland Greek New Testament

The New American Standard Bible (NASB) New Testament is keyed to the Nestle-Aland Greek New Testament. To move from an English word to its Greek equivalent using the NASB, do the following:

1. **Select the English word you want to study in Greek.** Open the NASB to John 1:1. Position the mouse cursor over the word "Word."

2. **Locate the Greek word from which the English was translated.** When you position the mouse cursor over many of the words in the NASB New Testament, the cursor has an asterisk (*) beside it. This indicates that there is an associated word link keyed to the word. To display this information, click the *right* mouse button on the word "Word," opening the right mouse menu. Click *Information* (⌐+I). A floating popup window opens, displaying the original Greek word, *logos*, and Strong's number, "3056."

3. **Open the Greek NT to the matching word in John 1:1.** Once again position the mouse cursor over the word "Word" in the NASB. Click the *right* mouse button on "Word," opening the right mouse menu. Click *Associated Word* (⌐+A). The Nestle-Aland Greek New Testament opens, displaying John 1:1 with *logos* highlighted (Fig. 8-4).

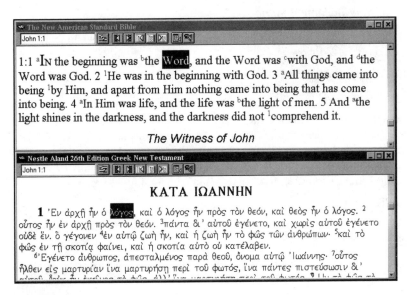

Figure 8-4 Nestle-Aland Greek NT Displays Associated Word from NASB.

4. **Use the lemma to locate appropriate articles on the word in Greek or Hebrew lexicons, dictionaries, etc.** To find the lemma for *logos*, click the

right mouse button on *logos,* opening the right mouse menu. Click *Information* (⌘+I). A floating popup window opens, displaying basic lexical information about *logos,* including the Greek lemma for this word, which in this case happens to be the same word, *logos.* Click the right mouse button on the lemma, *logos,* in the popup window, opening the right mouse menu. Click *KeyLink* (⌘+L). If you have properly set up KeyLink for Greek, the system should perform a Topic search, a Speed search, or open the Topic Browser on your favorite Greek lexicon (depending on how you defined the Greek KeyLink), locating appropriate articles. (For details on defining KeyLinks, see **Languages** in chapter seven, "System Management.")

Strong's Enhanced Lexicon

Following is an explanation of the information provided in an article in Strong's Enhanced Lexicon.

All lexicon entries are keyed to Strong's Numbers. The Greek lexicon is based on *Thayer's Lexicon* and *Smith's Bible Dictionary.* Where other sources were used, they are usually noted in the word definition. The Hebrew lexicon is based on *Brown Driver and Brigg's Lexicon* and *Gesenius Lexicon* with information from *Smith's Bible Dictionary.*

New Testament Entries

The information found in a New Testament (Greek) Strong's Number Lexicon entry is as follows:

- The transliterated Greek word.

- Phonetic spelling of the Greek word.

- Derivation information such as the volume and page numbers of Kittel's *Theological Dictionary of the New Testament* is displayed as "TDNT - ?" where the question mark represents a volume and page numbers, the first number referring to Kittel's *Dictionary,* the second number referring to Kittel's *Dictionary Abridged* (often known as "Little Kittel").

- The part of speech (noun, verb, etc.).

- The number of occurrences of each variant translation of the Greek word. This information is from the *Greek English Concordance* by J. B. Smith.

- If there are any synonyms for the Greek or Hebrew word, the number for the synonym(s) will be listed.

- The Goodrick & Kohlenberger number (a numbering scheme devised to improve on the original Strong's numbers), followed by the Greek lemma in parentheses.

- Lexical entries.

Old Testament Entries

The information found in an Old Testament (Hebrew) Strong's Number Lexicon entry is as follows:

- The key to the *Theological Wordbook of the Old Testament* is displayed as "TWOT - ?" where the question mark is an entry number in the Wordbook.

- The part of speech (noun, verb, etc.).

- For verbs, the Hebrew definitions contain the meanings for each Hebrew tense used in the Bible.

Hot Spot Numbers

Many Strong's lexicon entries contain references to other Strong's numbers which are displayed as highlighted Go To hot spots. When you position the cursor on a Go To hot spot, it will change to a hand cursor. Click the number and Strong's Lexicon will immediately jump to that lexical entry.

> NOTE: Return to the original entry by clicking the **Backtrack** button on the main Toolbar. (See **Bookmarks** in chapter three, "Viewing a Book.")

Strong's Number Search

Using Concordance search, you may search for Strong's numbers. Why search for Strong's numbers? If you search the KJV for the word "created," you will find 46 occurrences in Bible text. On the other hand, if you search for Strong's number 1254 (which represents the Hebrew word for "created"), you will find 54 occurrences in Bible text. Why the discrepancy? In some occasions of the Hebrew word for "created" the KJV translators translated it as "make" or "cut down." These occurrences will not be found by searching for "created."

To search for the Strong's number 1254:

1. Open the main Search dialog. Click the down arrow next to the Language box. Click Hebrew Strong's Numbers to select it. (Strong's numbers are considered to be a specific language, so that when you enter a Strong's number into the Search Query box, the system can distinguish this number from a regular number which could actually occur in a book's text.)

2. In the Search Query box enter the number 1254.

3. Change the Search Range to the KJV if necessary.

4. Click *Search*. NEBRL will search the KJV for all occurrences of the Hebrew Strong's Number 1254.

Greek and Hebrew Search

You may search a Greek or Hebrew text just as you would any English book.

When searching in a Greek or Hebrew Bible version, the text that you enter in the Search Query box must be in the proper language. NEBRL supplies Greek and Hebrew fonts. Use Windows Character Map (supplied with Microsoft Windows) to find the keyboard location of the desired Greek or Hebrew characters in these fonts.

Greek

To enter Greek words into the Search Query box:

- Click the *Greek* button next to the Languages box. (Or click the down arrow next to the Language box. Click Greek to select it.) When you enter text into the Search Query box, it will be in Greek. When you want to switch back to English (e.g., to enter a boolean operator), click the *English* button.

   NOTE: The English, Greek, and Hebrew buttons are provided as shortcuts because these are the three languages most often used in the Search Query box. However, any language on your system can be selected from the Languages drop-down list box.

   NOTE: When entering a Greek search query, it is not necessary to type the accents and breathing symbols for Greek words. This is because Greek-language searching ignores these diacritic marks.

Hebrew

To enter Hebrew words into the Search Query box:

- Click the *Hebrew* button next to the Languages box. (Or click the down arrow next to the Language box. Click Hebrew to select it.) When you enter text into the Search Query box, it will be in Hebrew, and it will enter from right to left because Hebrew reads from right to left. When you want to switch back to English (e.g., to enter a boolean operator), click the *English* button. As soon as you switch back to English, the text will resume entering from left to right.

   NOTE: When entering a Hebrew search query, it is not necessary to type the vowel markings or the Dagash consonant forms. This is because these diacritic marks are currently ignored in Hebrew-language searches (the Hebrew is treated as unpointed). Also, when searching Hebrew, you cannot mix concordance searches with phrase searches.

TVM Search

The TVM tab panel enables you to search the KJV according to the Tense, Voice, and Mood of the Greek and the Stem and Mood of the Hebrew based on the TVM numbering scheme tied to the KJV text. In other words, the Greek and Hebrew verbs in the original texts upon which the KJV is based, were each assigned a number based on their tense, voice, and mood. These numbers were then tied to the English translations of these verbs in the KJV. Therefore, without knowing Greek and Hebrew, you can search for verbs having a particular tense, voice, and mood.

Search Dialog TVM Search

To perform a TVM search from the main Search dialog:

1. Open the main Search dialog. Change the Search Range to the KJV and/or the Tense Voice Mood Lexicon if necessary. Among Bibles, you must use the KJV for a TVM search because it is the only Bible text which has the TVM numbers tied to the verbs. The TVM Lexicon is the only other book indexed according to the TVM numbers.

2. Click the TVM tab panel. In the Language box, click the Greek button. You are now able to select Tense, Voice, and Mood for Greek verbs.

3. Click Aorist to select a Tense. Click Active to select a Voice. Click Imperative to select a Mood. Click *Add* to add the TVM number to the Search Query box (Fig. 8-5). In this example the number will be 5657. This is the number that has been assigned to all Greek verbs which are Aorist Active Imperative.

4. Notice that the system has not only added the number 5657 to the Search Query box, but it has also added a space after it and changed the language back to English.

5. If you wish, you may add a boolean operator and another search word. For example, add "ANDEQUALS take."

6. Click *Search*. NEBRL will search the KJV for all occurrences of the TVM number 5657 tied to the verb "take," in other words, all cases where the English word "take" is a translation of a Greek verb in the Aorist Active Imperative.

   NOTE: Not all Tense/Voice/Mood and Stem/Mood combinations exist in the Bible or are even used at all. Therefore, some combinations will not have any matching TVM numbers. The *Add* button will be grayed in these instances and Matches will indicate 0.

You may also perform a search that is somewhat like a wildcard search. You may select a specific piece of verb information for one or more list

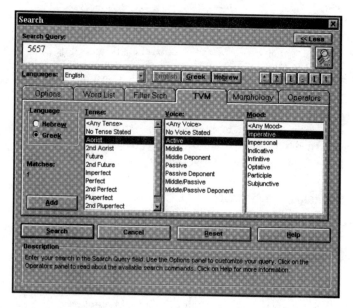

Figure 8-5 Search Dialog: TVM Search for Aorist Active Imperative Verbs.

boxes in the TVM tab panel, leaving one or two list boxes on the <Any> selection. This causes several TVM numbers to be filled into the Search dialog. (When working with Hebrew, you only have two list boxes, so you would be selecting only one specific piece of verb information, i.e., either the Stem or the Mood.)

For example, if you select Greek, then the 2nd Aorist Tense, Active voice, and any mood, six numbers surrounded by parentheses will be inserted into your search: "(5627 OR 5628 OR 5629 OR 5630 OR 5631 OR 5632)." Note that you must select at least one specific piece of verb information when using the TVM Search dialog.

Right Mouse TVM Search

To perform a TVM search using the right mouse menu:

1. In the KJV, position the mouse cursor over a verb. For example, go to Genesis 1:1 and position the cursor over the word "created."

2. The cursor has an asterisk (*) next to it, indicating that there is hidden information. With the cursor positioned on "created," click the right mouse button, opening the right mouse menu. Click *Information*. A popup window appears with the TVM number 8804.

3. Right-click on the TVM number 8804. From the right mouse menu, do either of the following:

- Select *KeyLink*. (You must have TVM keylinked to the TVM Lexicon, because it is the only book with TVM numbers assigned as Topics.) Selecting KeyLink on the TVM Lexicon can either perform a Topic search of the lexicon for all topics relating to 8804, or it can perform a full text search for all occurrences of the number 8804 in the lexicon. (For details on defining KeyLinks, see **Languages** in chapter seven, "System Management.")

- Select *Speed Search on Active Book*. NEBRL will search through the KJV for all occurrences of the number 8804 behind verbs.

Morphology Search

The Morphology tab panel enables you to search Greek and Hebrew texts according to parts of speech (Fig. 8-6).

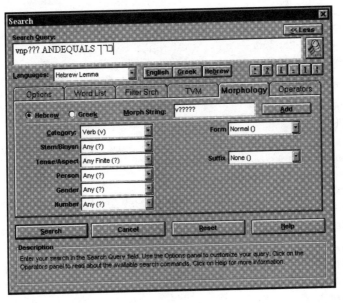

Figure 8-6 Search Dialog: Morphology Tab Panel.

The difference between the morphology feature and the TVM feature is twofold:

- Morphology includes the *full grammatical* information, or parsing, for *every* word; the full inflection is given (part of speech, gender, case, number, tense, voice, mood, etc.). TVM, on the other hand, includes only *partial* analyses of *verbs* (tense, voice, mood *only*).

- The morphology data is embedded in the morphologically-tagged NEBRL books: the Nestle-Aland Greek New Testament, the Septuagint, and the Biblia Hebraica Stuttgartensia Hebrew Old Testament. Each Greek or Hebrew word in the original texts is provided with its morphological information. The TVM data, on the other hand, is embedded in the King James Version. Each English verb is supplied with the TVM inflection code of the Greek or Hebrew word behind the translation.

To perform a morphology search from the main Search dialog:

1. Open the main Search dialog. Change the Search Range to the Nestle-Aland Greek NT, the Septuagint, or the Biblia Hebraica Stuttgartensia, as appropriate for your search. These are the three texts which have morphology data embedded with the text.

2. Click the Morphology tab panel. Click, for example, the Hebrew button. You are now able to select a Hebrew part of speech, and the appropriate categories for the part of speech.

3. Next to the Part of Speech box, click the down arrow and click Verb. The inflection boxes change to Stem/Binyan, Tense/Aspect, Person, Gender, Number, Form, and Suffix. Select Niphal Stem and Perfect Tense, leaving the other categories as wildcards. Click **Add** to add the Morphology acronym to the Search Query box (Fig. 8-6). In this example the morphology acronym will be "vnp???". This is the acronym that has been assigned to define Hebrew words which are Verb-Niphal-Perfect (no suffixes).

4. Notice that the system has not only added the acronym "vnp???" to the Search Query box, but it has also added a space after it and changed the language back to English.

5. If you wish, you may add a boolean operator and another search word. For example, add "ANDEQUALS *ûrb*"(Fig. 8-6). (After entering "AND-EQUALS", click **Hebrew Lemma** to change the language to Hebrew Lemma. Then enter *ûrb*.)

6. Click **Search**. NEBRL will search the Biblia Hebraica Stuttgartensia for all occurrences of the verb "to bless" where it occurs in the Niphal perfect (without suffixes).

9

Tips and Tricks

The following items have no user interface and are either too esoteric to be of general interest to NEBRL users or require editing of the LOGOS20.INI file (found in the Windows main directory). If you are comfortable editing the LOGOS20.INI file, carefully play with these items. Of course, it is advisable to backup the file before you edit it—just in case!

Wallpaper

NEBRL allows you to create a wallpaper for your NEBRL workspace. This wallpaper will appear in the area where you open books.

To use your favorite graphic image as your NEBRL wallpaper, do the following:

- In the [Preferences] section of LOGOS20.INI enter the following line:

    ```
    Wallpaper=c:\[path]\file.bmp
    ```

Placing a plus sign (+) after the equal sign (=) will cause small graphics to stagger their tiling on the screen.

Association Lists

Association lists enable the user to jump to a Bible verse which doesn't exist in the currently open Bible. For example, you have the Nestle-Aland Greek New Testament open on the screen. You jump to Genesis 3:15 which doesn't exist in the Greek New Testament. Where does NEBRL go? It jumps to the Bible which is "associated" with the Nestle-Aland Greek New Testament which, by default, is the BHS Hebrew Old Testament. Another example: In the KJV you jump to Tobit 1:1. The KJV Apocrypha will open automatically and appear in place of the KJV in the same window.

NEBRL automatically sets up the two above-mentioned associations for you when you install the software. To alter these or add others, you must edit LOGOS20.INI as follows:

```
NumAssociationLists=2
```

Replace the 2 with the total number of associations.

```
AssociatedTitles1=KJV,KJVAPOC
```

Change or add additional lines similar to the line above, incrementing the number 1 to 2 and so on. For the Bible names use the internal names, the ASCII names, or abbreviations of the book names. (The internal names can be found by looking at the directory of your books either on your hard drive or CD. The internal names precede the .LSF file extensions.)

Note that the association is used at the time of need only, and the first winner in the list is chosen. For example:

```
AssociatedTitles0=NA26,BHSMORPH

AssociatedTitles1=NA26,LXX
```

A jump from the LXX OT to the NT will open up NA26. However, a jump from NA26 to OT will go to the BHS, because it is first on the list.

For additional information, see **Navigating in a Book** in chapter three, "Viewing a Book."

ExecuteMacroDialog

The NEBRL macro language includes the command **ExecuteMacroDialog()**. This command opens a dialog which allows you to perform a one-time execution of any other NEBRL macro command conveniently from the main screen. To utilize this command:

■ Go to the Preferences dialog. Select Toolbar. Select a toolbar and then Customize. Select Properties, then Add Macro. The Add User Macro dialog opens. Create a new macro which executes the ExecuteMacroDialog command.

For example, in the Macro Name box you might type:

```
Execute Macro
```

The Macro Name is the text which shows up in the Macro button Tool Tip on the Toolbar.

In the Macro Text box, type:

```
ExecuteMacroDialog()
```

Click *OK*, returning to the Properties dialog. Assign a button to your new macro. Click *OK*, returning to the Customize Toolbar dialog. Move your new macro button onto your favorite Toolbar and then close the dialog.

Click on the new Toolbar button. A dialog will open allowing you to type any macro and execute it on the spot. For example, you might type:

```
SetScale(200)
```

This macro will increase the display size of your active book to 200% of its current size, doubling the type size.

StartupMacro

NEBRL will automatically execute the macro of your choice every time you start the software. For example, regardless of your saved workspace, every time you start NEBRL you want Spurgeon's *Morning and Evening* to open to the devotional for today. To do this, enter the following line into the [Preferences] section of LOGOS20.INI:

```
StartupMacro=OpenBook("Morning and
Evening");GoToToday(1)
```

Each time you start NEBRL, *Morning and Evening* will open to today's devotional.

Map File

What Is the Map File?

Following are details concerning the logos.map file which resides in your \lrsystem directory. This material should be used with *caution*. Most users should not have to manually edit this file, since the Title Librarian (found on the Tools Menu) handles the details of this file automatically. Be sure to make a copy of your logos.map file before you edit it—just in case!

The \lrsystem\logos.map file tells NEBRL in what directories to search for books and what books to either specifically load or specifically exclude.

The structure of the file is :

[Files]

path\book1.lsf

path\book1.lix

[Directories]

path\directory=

[Exclude]

book2.lsf=

[Files] Section

List .lsf and .lix files of books you want NEBRL to specifically load. This is useful if you want a particular version of the book to load from a specific location, or to see only the book you are working on in NEBRL.

To load a specific book, the path and file name of both the book and the index must be listed in the [Files] section (Example A).

Example A:

[Files]

c:\newbook\bhs.lsf

c:\newbook\bhs.lix

[Directories]

c:\logos20=

c:\lrsystem=

x:\Books= // Drive letter of the CD-ROM drive.

[Exclude]

nasb.lsf=

To load this book only and no other book, the book and index must be listed in the [Files] section, and the [Directories] section should contain the path of the LRSystem directory (Example B).

Example B:

[Files]

c:\newbook\bhs.lsf

c:\newbook\bhs.lix

[Directories]

c:\lrsystem=

If no books are listed in [Files], NEBRL will load the most recent versions of all unlocked books found in the directories listed in [Directories].

[Directories] Section

List pathnames of all directories containing NEBRL books here. Pathnames should be followed by =. NEBRL will search all these directories at startup for the newest available version of each unlocked book.

[Exclude] Section

List .lsf files of books you want NEBRL to exclude from loading. Filenames should be followed by =. Books can also be added to this section while in NEBRL from the Title Librarian dialog box in the Tools menu. This section can be used to specify that only a particular subset of unlocked books loads at startup.

Alternate Filemaps

You can run NEBRL with different filemaps by using the "/filemap" switch. This switch can be used either from the DOS prompt (Example C) or as an addition to the Command line for the icon in Win3.1 (Example D) or as an addition to the Target line for the shortcut icon in Win95 (Example E).

Example C:

c:\logos /filemap=<path of filemap>

Example: logos /filemap=c:\text\lsg.map

Example D:

Command Line (Win31): c:\logos20\logos.exe/filemap=<path of filemap>

Example E:

Target (Win95): c:\logos20\logos.exe /filemap=<path of filemap>

This alternate filemap is a **logos.map** file that contains a list of books that you do not want loaded. To create this map file, start by making a backup of your logos.map file. Then use the Title Librarian to remove the titles you don't want from the list of titles that are currently being loaded. This will create an [Exclude] section in your logos.map file that lists all of the titles that were removed with the Title Librarian. Finally, rename this new logos.map file to whatever custom name you desire and specify that file with the /filemap switch.

The new filemap will search through the directories listed in the [Directories] section of this custom logos.map file and load the most recent version of the unlocked books listed. (With the exception of the titles listed in the [Excludes] section, of course.) So, if you have a copy of an index on your local hard disk that is older than the same index on a network drive and both directories are listed in this [Directories] section, NEBRL will find and load the most recent version of the desired index.

A

The Bible

Books of the Bible and Their Abbreviations

Below is a list of all of the books in the Bible, the standard abbreviations used in NEBRL for these books, and the number of chapters in each book. Some Bible versions include the Apocrypha. This list also includes the books of the Apocrypha.

Specifying a Bible Passage

In order to specify a name, the user may type any of the abbreviations listed here. For example, if you want to specify Genesis 3:4, you may type:

```
Genesis 3:4, Gen 3:4, Ge 3:4, Gn 3:4, Genes 3:4
```

Also, there are a variety of ways to specify an enumerated book. For example, you may type any of the following for 2 Kings:

```
2 Kings, II Kings, Second Kings, 2nd Kings
```

Also, the spaces are optional. You may type:

```
1 Sam 1:3 or 1Sam1:3
```

If you want to go to verse one of Psalms chapter 8, the verse number is unnecessary. You may type:

```
Ps 8:1 or Ps 8
```

To go to chapter 1, verse 1 of Psalms, type either:

```
Ps 1:1 or Ps
```

Finally, you may use a colon (:), a semicolon (;), or a period (.) as the chapter/verse delimiter. You may type either:

```
Ps 8:30, Ps 8;30, or Ps 8.30
```

Old Testament	Medium Form	Short Form	Extra Forms	Chapters
Genesis	Gen	Ge	Gn	50
Exodus	Exo	Ex	Exod	40
Leviticus	Lev	Le		27
Numbers	Num	Nu		36
Deuteronomy	Deut	Dt	Deu, De	34
Joshua	Josh	Jos		24
Judges	Judg	Jdg		21
Ruth	Rth	Ru		4
1 Samuel	1 Sam	1 Sa		31
2 Samuel	2 Sam	2 Sa		24

1 Kings	1 Kgs	1 Ki		22
2 Kings	2 Kgs	2 Ki		25
1 Chronicles	1 Chron	1 Ch		29
2 Chronicles	2 Chron	2 Ch		36
Ezra	Ezra	Ezr		10
Nehemiah	Neh	Ne		13
Esther	Esth	Es	Est	10
Job	Job	Job		42
Psalm	Pslm	Ps	Psa, Psm, Pss, Psalms	150
Proverbs	Prov	Pr	Pro	31
Ecclesiastes	Eccles	Ec	Ecc, Qoh, Qoheleth	12
Song of Solomon	Song	So	Son, Song of Songs, SOS, SS, Canticles of Canticles, Canticles	8
Isaiah	Isa	Is		66
Jeremiah	Jer	Je		52
Lamentations	Lam	La	Lament	5
Ezekiel	Ezek	Eze		48
Daniel	Dan	Da		12
Hosea	Hos	Ho		14
Joel	Joel	Joe		3
Amos	Amos	Am	Amo	9
Obadiah	Obad	Ob	Oba	1
Jonah	Jnh	Jon		4
Micah	Micah	Mic		7
Nahum	Nah	Na		3
Habakkuk	Hab	Hab		3
Zephaniah	Zeph	Zep		3
Haggai	Haggai	Hag		2
Zechariah	Zech	Zec		14
Malachi	Mal	Mal		4

New Testament	*Medium Form*	*Short Form*	*Extra Forms*	*Chapters*
Matthew	Matt	Mt	Mat	28
Mark	Mrk	Mk	Mar, Mr	16
Luke	Luk	Lk	Lu	24
John	John	Jn	Joh	21
Acts	Acts	Ac	Act	28
Romans	Rom	Ro		16
1 Corinthians	1 Cor	1 Co		16
2 Corinthians	2 Cor	2 Co		13
Galatians	Gal	Ga		6
Ephesians	Ephes	Eph		6
Philippians	Phil	Php	Phi	4
Colossians	Col	Col		4
1 Thessalonians	1 Thess	1 Th	1 Thes	5
2 Thessalonians	2 Thess	2 Th	2 Thes	3
1 Timothy	1 Tim	1 Ti		6
2 Timothy	2 Tim	2 Ti		4

Titus	Titus	Tit		3
Philemon	Philem	Phm		1
Hebrews	Hebrews	Heb		13
James	James	Jas	Jam	5
1 Peter	1 Pet	1 Pe		5
2 Peter	2 Pet	2 Pe		3
1 John	1 John	1 Jn	1 Jo, 1 Joh	5
2 John	2 John	2 Jn	2 Jo, 2 Joh	1
3 John	3 John	3 Jn	3 Jo, 3 Joh	1
Jude	Jude	Jud		1
Revelation	Rev	Re	The Revelation	22

Apocrypha	Medium Form	Short Form	Extra Forms	Chapters
Tobit	Tobit	Tob		14
Judith	Jdth	Jdt		16
Additions to Esther	Add Esth	Add Es	The Rest of Esther, Rest of Esther, AEs	16
Wisdom of Solomon	Wisd of Sol	Wis	The Wisdom of Solomon, Wisd of Sol, Wisdom	19
Sirach	Sirach	Sir		51
Baruch	Baruch	Bar		5
Letter of Jeremiah	Let Jer	Let Jer	Ltr Jer, LJe	1
Song of Three Jews	Song of Three	Song Thr	The Song of the Three Holy Children, The Song of Three Jews, Song of the Three Holy Children, Song of Thr, Song of Three Children, Prayer of Azariah, Azariah, Pr Az	1
Susanna	Susanna	Sus		1
Bel and the Dragon	Bel	Bel		1
1 Maccabees	1 Macc	1 Mac	1 Ma	16
2 Maccabees	2 Macc	2 Mac	2 Ma	15
1 Esdras	1 Esdr	1 Esd	1 Es	9
Prayer of Manasseh	Pr of Man	Pr Man	Prayer of Manasses, PMa	1
Additional Psalm	Add Psalm	Add Ps		1
3 Maccabees	3 Macc	3 Mac	3 Ma	7
2 Esdras	2 Esdr	2 Esd	2 Es	16
4 Maccabees	4 Macc	4 Mac	4 Ma	18
Ode	Ode	Ode		1
Psalms of Solomon	Ps Solomon	Ps Sol	Psalms Solomon, PsSol	1

Using the Apocrypha

In NEBRL, the Apocrypha is found between the Old and New Testaments, except for the King James Version where the Apocrypha is a separate book.

The Apocryphal book "Letter of Jeremiah" is a one-chapter book, but its first chapter is 6. However, you do not need to remember this or specify chapter 6 when referring to the book. If you type *Let Jer 12,* you will end up in Letter of Jeremiah, chapter 6, verse 12.

Some Bibles refer to the Apocryphal book "Additional Psalm" as "Psalm 151," but in order to differentiate between the book of "Psalms" and "Psalm 151," NEBRL calls it "Additional Psalm." Also, this book is much like Letter of Jeremiah in that it is a one-chapter book whose first chapter is not chapter one.

Bible Versions

Over the years several Bible versions have been created. Each one has had a slightly different translation philosophy behind it which has affected the way in which it was translated.

Some Bibles, like the King James Version, the New King James Version, the American Standard Version 1901, and the New American Standard Bible, are called *literal* translations. The purpose of a literal translation is to convey the word-for-word meaning of the original Greek and Hebrew manuscripts as closely as the English language will allow.

Some Bibles, like the New International Version, are called *dynamic equivalent* translations. The purpose of a dynamic equivalent translation is to convey the thought behind the text as opposed to the word-for-word meaning of the text.

Some Bible versions come with additional text such as chapter titles, article titles, translator's notes, etc. The *Nelson Electronic Bible Reference Library* allows you to display only the Bible text or to include the additional text of the printed version if you so desire.

B

Keyboard Shortcuts

Most NEBRL features can be accessed from the Menu Bar by using the mouse or by holding down the ALT key and pressing the underlined letter of the menu option desired. There are also a number of **Keyboard Shortcuts** designed to help experienced users more quickly do their work.

Keystroke	Description
Up Arrow	Scroll the window text back toward the beginning of the article.
Down Arrow	Scroll the window text forward toward the end of the article.
Left Arrow	View the previous Bible version in the active document window. The list of available Bible versions is found in the Library Browser.
Right Arrow	View the next Bible version in the active document window. The list of available Bible versions is found in the Library Browser.
PgUp	Move up a window-full of text.
PgDn	Move down a window-full of text.
Shift+PgUp	In Bibles, move to the beginning of the current chapter, or to the beginning of the previous chapter if at the beginning already.
Shift+PgDn	In Bibles, move to the beginning of the next chapter.
Ctrl+PgUp	In Bibles, move to the beginning of the current book, or to the beginning of the previous book if at the beginning already.
Ctrl+PgDn	In Bibles, move to the beginning of the next book.
Ctrl+Shift+>	Make text larger in current document window.
Ctrl+Shift+<	Make text smaller in current document window.
Alt+Enter	Display Information Pop-Up behind highlighted word.
F1	Display context-sensitive Help.
F5	Open a new Bible window.
Ctrl+F5	Open the New Bible Window and Reference dialog.
Ctrl+B	Toggle the Library Browser on and off.
Ctrl+C	Copy selected text from the current location onto the Windows clipboard.
Ctrl+F	Open the Search dialog. This is equivalent to pressing the **Search** button on the Toolbar.
Ctrl+G	Highlight the current reference inside the Scripture Reference Box. Type a new reference and from the keyboard press ENTER to go there.
Ctrl+N	Create new note file.

Ctrl+O	Open the File Open dialog.
Ctrl+P	Open the Print dialog.
Ctrl+Q	Quit NEBRL.
Ctrl+R	When the active document window is displaying a book which has Bible references indexed for it, CTRL + R opens the Reference Browser.
Ctrl+S	Save the note file in the active document window.
Ctrl+V	Paste the text from the Windows clipboard into the current document.
Ctrl+W	Open the Global Word List window.
Ctrl+X	Cut selected text from the current location onto the Windows clipboard.
Ctrl+Y	Sync Browser with current text location.
Ctrl+Z	Undo previous changes.

C

DDE Support

This Appendix is intended only for those technically proficient in working with Dynamic Data Exchange (DDE). We are supplying the information necessary for technical users to communicate with NEBRL utilizing DDE.

NEBRL supports only one Service name: "Logos." The following topics and items are available for use with the given DDE commands. For information on executing DDE commands, see the Windows Software Development Kit or the reference manual for the DDE-aware application you'll be using with NEBRL. All parameters and return values are strings. Upper case is used for parameters that are required and return values, lower case is used for optional parameters. An "S," or "s" indicates that the value should be interpreted as a string of text, an "N," or "n" indicates that the value should be interpreted as a string form of an integer number, a "B," or "b" indicates the value should be interpreted as a Boolean which can be a "0," or "FALSE" for false, or "1," or "TRUE" for true.

Topics:

System   The system topic is a general topic that provides global services on the application that are usually common to other applications. All services in the system topic are available from all other topics unless that topic has a service with the same name as one in the system topic.

Info   The info topic provides specific information about data in inside the application.

Search   The search topic provides access to various types of search related features inside Logos.

Text   The text topic provides services relating to retrieval of data inside the application.

Command   The command topic gives the application general commands to perform.

Syntax for Services:

Execute Services

[<Command> (<Parameter1>, <Parameter2>, ...)][Command (<Parameter1>, <Parameter2>, ...] ...

<Command>   Indicates the name of the execute service.

<ParameterX>   Indicate a string representing the data to be passed as a parameter to <Command>. There may be a minimum number of required pa-

rameters as well as several optional parameters to each service. All parameters to the left of the last optional parameter are required. Consult the documentation on the individual services.

Note: Many execute services can be used in the same execute string as indicated above. Example: an execute on the "Search" topic might be "[Activate][Concordance(Peace)]." The "Activate" service would be used from the "System" topic, then the "Concordance" service would be used in the "Search" topic.

Execute services do not return data.

Request Services

\<Item\> (\<Parameter1\>, \<Parameter2\>, ...)

\<Item\>   Indicates the name of the request service.

\<ParameterX\>   Indicate a string representing the data to be passed as a parameter to \<Item\>. There may be a minimum number of required parameters as well as several optional parameters to each service. All parameters to the left of the last optional parameter are required. Consult the documentation on the individual services.

Note: Unlike the execute, only one request may be made at a time because each service will return data to the caller.

The System Topic:

Execute Services

Minimize
>   Minimizes the application

Maximize
>   Maximizes the application

Activate
>   Activates the application

SetWindowPos(N, N, N, N, N, N)
>   Sets the position of the application window.
>>   Parameter 1: Handle of the window to insert after. This can be an actual window handle or one of the following values.
>>>   "0"= Top
>>>   "1"= Bottom
>>>   "-1"= Topmost
>>>   "-2"= NoTopmost
>>   Parameter 2: X Position in pixels.
>>   Parameter 3: Y Position in pixels.
>>   Parameter 4: X Width in pixels.
>>   Parameter 5: Y Width in pixels.

Parameter 6: Window positioning flags can be any combination of the following values. These values must be combined with a binary OR operation before they are sent.

0x0001 = SWP_NOSIZE

0x0002 = SWP_NOMOVE

0x0004 = SWP_NOZORDER

0x0008 = SWP_NOREDRAW

0x0010 = SWP_NOACTIVATE

0x0020 = SWP_FRAMECHANGED

0x0040 = SWP_SHOWWINDOW

0x0080 = SWP_HIDEWINDOW

0x0100 = SWP_NOCOPYBITS

0x0200 = SWP_NOOWNERZORDER

0x0400 = SWP_NOSENDCHANGING

0x2000 = SWP_DEFERERASE

Consult the documentation for the Windows SDK SetWindowPos function for more details.

Request Services

(S) Topics

Returns a tab delimited list of the topics supported by this server

(S) Items

Returns a tab delimited list of the items under this topic. This item is automatically overloaded in each topic in the server.

(S) ReturnMessage

Returns a description of the last operation.

(S) Version

Returns a string representing the version of this software.

The Info Topic

Request Services

(N) NumBooks

Returns: The number of books loaded.

(N) BookNum(S)

Returns the number of a book by its name.

Parameter 1:   The name of the book for which the number is requested. The name can be either the full ASCII name or the internal name.

Returns: The book number.

(S) BookName(N)

Returns the ASCII name of the book.

Parameter 1: The number of the book for which the name is requested.

Returns: The ASCII name of the book.

(N) CurBook

Returns: The number of the current book.

(S) CurBookName

Returns: The ASCII name of the current book.

(S) CurBookAbr

Returns: The internal abbreviated name of the current book.

(N) NumBibles

Returns: The number of Bibles loaded.

(N) BibleNum(S)

Parameter 1: The name of the book for which the number is requested. The name can be either the full ASCII name or the internal name.

Returns: The Bible number.

(S) BibleName(N)

Parameter 1: The number of the book for which the name is requested.

Returns: The ASCII name of the Bible.

(N) CurBible

Returns: The number of the current Bible.

(S) CurBibleName

Returns: The ASCII name of the current Bible.

(S) CurBibleAbr

Returns: The internal abbreviated name of the current Bible.

(N) NumCategories

Returns: The number of categories loaded.

(N) NumSubcategories(N)

Parameter 1: The number of the category for which the number of subcategories is requested.

Returns: The number of subcategories loaded.

(N) CategoryNum(S)

Parameter 1: The name of the category for which the number is requested.

Returns: The number of the category.

(S) CategoryName(N)

Parameter 1: The number of the category for which the name is requested.

Returns: The name of the category.

(N) SubCategoryNum(N, S)

Parameter 1: The number of the category which contains the category name in Parameter 2.

Parameter 2: The name of the subcategory for which the number is requested.

Returns: The number of the subcategory.

(S) SubCategoryName(N, N)

Parameter 1:   The number of the category which contains the category in Parameter 2.

Parameter 2:   The number of the subcategory for which the name is requested.

Returns: The name of the subcategory.

(S) FullReference(S)

Parameter 1:   The verse reference or passage for which the fully expanded reference is requested.

Returns: The fully expanded form of the verse reference or passage.

The Search Topic

Execute Services

SetRange(S, s)

Sets the range for the next search only.

Parameter 1:   Book Range. The books may be either the full ASCII names or their internal names separated by a vertical bar " | ".

Parameter 2:   Verse Range. The verse ranges may be any combination of passages separated by a semicolon ";".

Concordance(S, s, s)

Performs a concordance search.

Parameter 1:   The text to be searched.

Parameter 2:   The name of the language that describes Parameter 1. The default for this parameter if it is not used is "English."

Parameter 3:   The name of the font used to encode the text in Parameter 1. The default for this parameter if it is not used is "Times New Roman." This parameter is important to determine the meaning of the characters of Parameter 1. Different fonts often place the representation of a character in different positions. For instance the Greek letter beta appears at position 223 in the Times New Roman font while in the SemiticaDict font it appears at position 167, yet they are semantically the same.

Phrase(S, s, s)

Performs a phrase search.

Parameter 1:   The text to be searched.

Parameter 2:   The name of the language that describes Parameter 1. The default for this parameter if it is not used is "English."

Parameter 3:   The name of the font used to encode the text in Parameter 1. The default for this parameter if it is not used is "Times New Roman." This parameter is important to determine the meaning of the characters of Parameter 1. Different fonts often place the representation of a character in different positions. For instance the

Greek letter beta appears at position 223 in the Times New Roman font while in the SemiticaDict font it appears at position 167, yet they are semantically the same.

KeyWord(S, s, s)

Performs a keyword search.

Parameter 1:   The text to be searched.

Parameter 2:   The name of the language that describes Parameter 1. The default for this parameter if it is not used is "English."

Parameter 3:   The name of the font used to encode the text in Parameter 1. The default for this parameter if it is not used is "Times New Roman." This parameter is important to determine the meaning of the characters of Parameter 1. Different fonts often place the representation of a character in different positions. For instance the Greek letter beta appears at position 223 in the Times New Roman font while in the SemiticaDict font it appears at position 167, yet they are semantically the same.

Ref(S)

Performs a reference search.

Parameter 1:   The verse reference or passage to be searched.

KeyLink(S, s, s)

Performs a keylink.

Parameter 1:   The text to be keylinked.

Parameter 2:   The name of the language that describes Parameter 1. The default for this parameter if it is not used is "English."

Parameter 3:   The name of the font used to encode the text in Parameter 1. The default for this parameter if it is not used is "Times New Roman." This parameter is important to determine the meaning of the characters of Parameter 1. Different fonts often place the representation of a character in different positions. For instance the Greek letter beta appears at position 223 in the Times New Roman font while in the SemiticaDict font it appears at position 167, yet they are semantically the same.

DefineKeyLink(S, S, n, b, b)

Redefines a keylink.

Parameter 1:   The name of the language for which this link operation is to be defined.

Parameter 2:   The name of the book to which to link the language in Parameter 1. The name can be either the full ASCII name or the internal name.

Parameter 3:   The type of link this operation should be.

"0" = Key word browser

"1" = Key word search

"2" = Concordance search

Parameter 4:   Prepend wildcard. This will automatically add a "*" wild card to the front of the text sent in a key link in the language of Parameter 1.

Parameter 5   Append wildcard. This will automatically add a "*" wild card to the end of the text sent in a key link in the language of Parameter 1.

The Text Topic

Execute Services

Copy (S, S)

Copies text to the clipboard in all possible formats.

Parameter 1:   The name of the book in which the text is to be found. The name can be the full ASCII name or the internal name.

Parameter 2:   The passage requested.

Note: This service currently supports only texts that are organized by biblical reference, including Bibles and Commentaries.

The Command Topic

Execute Services

Open(S)

Opens a book in the workspace.

Parameter 1:   The name of the book requested. The name can be the full ASCII name or the internal name.

Close

Closes the active book.

CloseAll

Closes all books in the workspace.

Goto(S)

Opens an article in a book.

Parameter 1:   The context of the article to be loaded.

GotoContext(S)

Opens an article in a book.

Parameter 1:   The context of the article to be loaded.

GotoReference(S)

Opens a Bible to a verse reference.

Parameter 1:   The verse reference of the passage to be loaded.